Financial
Intervention

Financial Intervention

Creating Money for Life

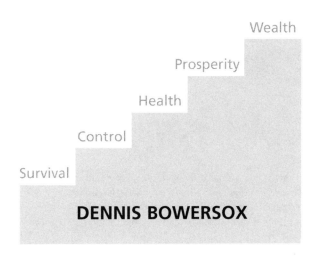

Wealth

Prosperity

Health

Control

Survival

DENNIS BOWERSOX

This publication is designed to provide accurate and authoritative information in regard to the subject matter covered. It is sold with the understanding that the publisher is not engaged in rendering legal, accounting, or other professional service. If legal or other professional advice is required, the services of a competent professional should be sought.

Published by Financial Health Systems, LLC, 1-800-974-5870

Web site: www.creatingmoneyforlife.com

Copyright © 2007 Dennis Bowersox

All rights reserved. No part of this publication may be reproduced or transmitted in any form or by any means, electronic or mechanical, including photocopy, recording, or any information storage and retrieval system, without permission in writing from the publisher.

I am dedicating this book:

> *To my loving wife Laui for a wonderful 39 years and for her patience and support all these years of my being an entrepreneur and real estate investor. We grew together through the ups and downs of many ventures that provided me the streetsmart education to pass on to those who desire change.*

> *To my daughter Blair who works with me and took on the responsibility of the day-to-day management of the Real Estate Investing and Bankruptcy Debtor Education Company, which allowed me the time to write this book.*

> *To my other two daughters, Bree and her husband Eric Hansen, and Corry and her husband Eric Monroe for being the productive, prosperous, successful, and happy adults they are, which allowed me the emotional comfort to be able to focus on creating this publication.*

Contents

Acknowledgments

I want to thank in advance the purchasers of this book who will use it to take charge of their financial futures, to change their actions, and to avoid becoming stressed, financial victims. I especially want the users of this book to pass it on to future generations—to their children, other relatives, and friends, breaking the cycle of dependence on debt and social security.

Introduction

I have written this book to share my many years of experience with helping people develop their personal financial-management skills. I enjoy helping others get on a new path toward creating money for the rest of their lives. During the last ten years I have been working with people who have bad credit, are struggling financially, are frustrated with their debt load, have lost their home to foreclosure or are going through bankruptcy. I feel good about helping them, but I also want to help the financially healthy become financially wealthy.

When meeting people I don't know, I am frequently asked what I do for a living. I tell them that I own a company that helps people stop living paycheck to paycheck and teaches them how to create the financial future they want. On saying that, I typically get the response: "I need that." It reinforces what the media often say: Many Americans need help. The question is, will they do anything before it is too late? The results we seek are to have anyone who admits needing help with their finances become financially healthy and wealthy.

This book is a great guide for those struggling financially. It also can be of great importance to those who see themselves as financially healthy today but are not preparing for their needs when their earned income stops.

I want to thank you for caring enough about your financial future to buy this book. It will help you get a clear picture of where you are financially in reference to the Five Financial Lifestyles. It will show you how to stop struggling with money issues and remove the fear of retiring in poverty—starting today. The information will show you how to quickly get off the path of destruction and on the right track for financial growth. My goal is to help those who want to grow into a life of financial peace and prosperity. This book can be your guide, helping you create the income you need—forever.

This book works well as a diagnostic tool to match your financial habits with the behaviors/characteristics of those living other lifestyles. You will be able to determine which lifestyle you are living, whether or not you are stuck in that lifestyle, and what new behaviors you will need to assimilate in order to insure financial growth.

According to *The Wall Street Journal,* 70 percent of Americans are only one paycheck away from not being able to pay their bills. A recent Associated Press report said that personal savings in the United States have dropped to a 74-year low. In other words, savings rates are at their worst since the Great Depression in 1933.

Considering the high percentage of Americans who are or soon will be in financial trouble, now is the time to intervene. We Americans have amassed more than $1 trillion in consumer debt. This is a major problem and I would like to be part of the solution. I want to help prevent people from going bankrupt or being foreclosed upon. Most people are on autopilot financially—heading for a disastrous future. They live paycheck to paycheck. What do you think will happen when they no longer get a paycheck? I want to get the public's attention and say "Wake up!" before they fall into the "no money for retirement" ditch.

Many Americans have approached their finances by trial and error. They never had any financial management training and they haven't acquired the knowledge or skills to take control and make the changes needed to advance financially. Without help, they can't change their focus or mind-set, or the way they manage their money. Without changing what they are doing, they will stay in their current lifestyle and continue to get the same results. Even worse, they don't know where to get help. People need to take different actions and face new challenges on every level. Financial management guidance is needed to help them move from living at or below their means to having a bright financial future. Except for a few books, CDs, speakers, and home-study courses, the information and tools needed for change are not available. By learning to use only a few of the necessary tools, such as a budget, and changing a few behaviors, people think they have made major accomplishments. The truth is, without totally changing how people behave and manage their money, they will only experience a slight improvement. Their gain will be so slow that they will not be redirecting their financial future and will only see a temporary advancement. Often they slip back. After reading this book you will understand that in order to become healthy, prosperous or wealthy, you will need many adjustments. I have discovered more than 80 actions taken by people who grow through the 5 lifestyles from survival to wealth. Thus, if you only adopt a few of theses actions you will only get minor results. You will be better off financially than you were when you started, but won't ever reach the wealthy lifestyle.

Do you remember when you took driver's training? You needed to be taught how to drive the car safely. The instructor taught you in proper sequence. What if he or she had you get on a highway the first day of training, going 70 miles per hour to teach you how to use the cruise control? If you weren't first taught how to steer and brake, you would be in trouble and you might soon crash. Without financial intervention, that is exactly what will happen financially to 70 percent of Americans. Are you heading directly into the financial ditch? If so, you can intervene now and change your direction.

The problem is that many people rely on one of four belief systems when it comes to improving their finances. Those who are so focused on today don't know where they are heading. Like someone walking into the shallow end of a swimming pool—they feel safe and comfortable even if they are approaching the deep end. If they don't know how to change from walking to swimming, they will soon be in trouble.

Being comfortable is a financial hazard also. Many people are just getting by today and see the future as being a long, long way away. Or, like the ostrich they put their heads in the sand and hope their finances will straighten out on their own. Others have the lottery mentality and keep spending, hoping to win soon and solve their problems. In the sales mind-set, people feel they can always outearn the money they need. They buy, hoping for a better future. Be honest with yourself. Do any of these four scenarios apply to you? If not, that's great. The next question for you then is: "Do you a want a future of wealth?" Whatever your answer, keep reading!

Most people are stuck in a survival lifestyle. This means living at a level at their means and barely getting by. However, many people, through trial and error, can develop the skills to achieve a healthy lifestyle—defined as living within their means and having a little extra money at the end of the month. But those on the healthy level aren't saving or investing enough to ever retire with financial security or stay comfortable.

My parents lived in the healthy financial lifestyle all of their lives. For the most part my mother was a stay at home mom. My father worked in the accounting department of a large paper manufacturing company. He was not highly paid but made enough to create a comfortable life. My parents were always very frugal. Our needs were always met and we did take vacations and much of my brother and my undergraduate college expenses were paid for.

They are perfect examples of those living the healthy lifestyle. They controlled their money and never wasted it. Until my father turned 94 and my mother 88, they were fine financially. My dad has been retired for 32 years. They went to Florida many winters and enjoyed lots of card games with friends. They didn't spend a lot of money, they were happy. They were extremely good with handling their money. Without knowing it they were stuck in the Healthy lifestyle. Getting stuck happens to most people because they don't have the education from which to make behavior changes. I hope this book will give a new insight on where people stand financially, where they need to be and how to get there. This book can help them change. My father has told me more than once that he hasn't paid any interest for over 40 years. That is a real accomplishment!

The problems came about when my mother fell and broke her hip and ended up in a nursing home. Their financial freedom and ability to get what they want financially ended at that point in time. The level of health care my mother needs is twenty four hours a day seven days a week. That is the only way she can come home so they can be together for the rest of their lives. After 68 years together that is what they want and deserve.

The cost of the nursing home that she is currently in is $6,000 per month. If she goes home the bill goes to $12,000 a month. The home care will not be covered by medicare or medicaid and they would have to pay it from their savings. Living the healthy lifestyle, they never accumulated a large net worth. The money isn't there to cover that level of expense.

Here is where they got hurt by living in the healthy lifestyle. They could have lived out their lives comfortably financially if the health problems didn't occur. Make sure you check if you want to use this book to become wealthy or make sure you have enough long term care insurance.

With my parents not paying any interest for forty years, their situation could be different. You would think being frugal and a great money manager all your life would be sufficient. It might not be!

There are three financial strategies to handle your money when you are in the healthy lifestyle. Forty years ago a house payment and car payment would have been around $500. There were no credit cards at that time.

If you took the $500 a month and put it into CD's or Savings accounts you would accumulate approximately $295,192. This is the frugal and safe way, as my parents did. Considering that, with CD and savings account rates you are only getting about 1% return after you deduct for inflation. If you factor in a 6% income stream from low risk mutual funds or municipal bonds you would get $1,476 a month after accumulating the $295,192. That doesn't come close to the $12,000 just for caregivers costs.

If you grow to the prosperity level you would most likely have invested in the stock market at an average return of 8 percent. Forty years of $500 a month at 8 percent after deducting 3% for inflation would provide you with a net worth of

$766,189. That would generate $3,831 per month at 6% fairly safe return. Still not enough to cover nursing care.

If you decided to keep growing to the wealthy lifestyle you would have invested in real estate or businesses. Let's take real estate at 20 percent return. Take away the 3 percent for inflation and your net worth would be $30,604,372. That net worth, at our 6% conservative investing, would bring you $153,022 per month.

Even though these are hypothetical examples, I think you can see the difference. Even if you didn't have all forty years due to eliminating debt, cover some bad investing decisions and losses you would still be in great financial shape if you avoided being stuck in the healthy lifestyle and went for the gold.

Those living the healthy lifestyle will most likely stay there and won't progress, simply because they don't have the knowledge or tools to make the adjustments that foster change. This book will give you both the knowledge and the tools to guide you to a wealthy lifestyle.

I'll guarantee you have never heard of or used many of these street-smart, easy-to-use techniques—especially if you activate the lessons through a step by step process. This is the only way you will progress through each level and reach the wealthy lifestyle in a reasonable time frame. The tools will work for you starting at your current income level. Contrary to popular belief, you don't need money to make money. You just need education and the drive to use it to intervene. This applies no matter what your current finanial lifestyle.

Through my experience of working with people at all financial levels, I have discovered everyone is living in one of five financial lifestyles. This book will give you the information and show you how to progress through each lifestyle. Your lifestyle is determined by the way you think and function with your money. It is not based on income level, winning the lottery, or your level of formal education. These tools will help you change your mind-set, focus, and behaviors, which will put you on the path to a higher financial lifestyle. Using this different approach to the way you think and deal with your money, you will be able to create wonderful results. You will read how the wealthy think and act differently from those who are merely surviving.

If you have the desire and will commit to using the knowledge and tools, you can quickly elevate your financial well-being. You will also learn about the challenges or roadblocks you will have to face and overcome in order to progress. Another aspect to consider is to make sure you enjoy the rewards that come with each lifestyle. Those benefits will help reinforce and sustain your efforts.

There is a major difference between those who just survive and those who are wealthy. The good news is that anyone can learn to become financially free. Because the skills needed to be a great financial manager are learned behaviors, you can reach any level you set your mind to. The skills are not gained through heredity or environment. They are learned. I have seen people who grew up in a wealthy home become adults who live the survival lifestyle. Have you heard of the rich son or daughter who blew an inheritance? To be highly successful you must learn the process in sequence. Of course you must also take the appropriate actions.

Those who become successful in the shortest time, while advancing from survival to wealth, incorporate the following patterns. They quickly learn to control their money "leaks." When that is accomplished they set up their advanced control plans and systems. From there they allocate 100 percent of their income to these categories: expense and debt payments;

set-aside account reserves; and allowance. When these systems function they will be able to find extra money for their debt-elimination program. Once the debt-elimination plan is working properly they can move on to investing to build wealth. In following this pattern they will always be placing their money where it needs to be to accelerate debt elimination and enhance investment growth.

With all monies accounted for you will be able to stay on track for debt elimination and investing, allowing you to reach whatever financial goals you desire. Without allocating all income, leaks will occur, and you will grow old and not have a clue where all your money went.

You will learn new information and the activities needed to redirect your focus; change your buying habits; begin to operate from plans; move from emotional to logical spending; clean up your credit; get out of bad debt; invest wisely and protect your assets. If it sounds like a lot of work—it is. But knowing it will give you a future of financial freedom and peace makes it all worthwhile.

The process is simple but not easy. It is never too late to make a change. The sooner you start the easier it is and the faster you will reap the rewards. Please start now so you can improve your financial situation and have a money-filled future. Most people don't realize they are letting others control their money. Most people make more than a million dollars during their lifetime. Very few can tell you where it went, nor if they used it wisely to create passive income. When you take full control, you can have fun saving and investing and not be locked into looking at your job as needed income forever. You will have your money working for you rather than you working for your money. Once your money is working for you, you will be able to relax. Who wants to have to flip burgers at age 70?

You will know how to make the right adjustments to handling your money, and this will put you on the path to financial freedom. The goal is to get out of debt and to create passive income to replace your earned income. You will learn to recognize exactly where you are financially, the reasons you are not advancing, and a step-by-step attitude and behavior change for each financial level.

This book will walk you through the five financial lifestyles and teach you the lessons you need to be successful. It will also provide the tools you will need for taking action. However, you will have to create the passion to overcome the challenges at each level. The rewards along the way will give you energy to keep moving forward. The lessons, tools, and actions will keep you on track so you will attract all the money you want for life. If you decide you want more out of your financial life—go for it. The lifestyle you want to live is totally up to you. Changing lifestyles is a matter of learning new behaviors. With some effort you can create the financial future you want. But you will have to intervene by getting the education and taking the right actions. My company staff will be available to support and help you all the way. We offer group face to face and teleseminars, home study courses and one on one coaching in personal finance and Real Estate investing classes and consulting. Our approach starts with getting to know the clients current situation and what they want to achieve. We start by listening and asking questions in a caring atmosphere. From there we guide them through the steps to become financially successful. If you want to take the shortcut to wealth contact us at *www.creatingmoneyforlife.com.*

You deserve more! Read, enjoy, learn to think differently and take the necessary actions to sustain growth and get the results you want. It's up to you! You can do it!

Chapter **ONE**

The Six Missions

I have written this book to help achieve many results. There are six main goals or missions.

Mission One—To help you come to some comparative accurate conclusions. First, you must match your current knowledge level with what you need to know about your own finances to compare your current success level. Second, match your current financial behaviors against the behaviors with those in the high level lifestyle as presented in this book with what you could be doing for a more secure financial future. Third, realize what lifestyle you are living. Decide if you want to live a different level or style. Measure your current net worth against where you should be to have the money necessary for retirement.

Part of the reason for writing this book is to get you to honestly and openly admit to yourself that you are not as financially healthy as you would like to be. It will also help you follow the correct path to financial growth in order to avoid being sidetracked or ending up in the ditch. Most people think they are in control and are doing all right. This is because they have nothing to compare with or are living in denial.

With some education and intervention you will see there is a different world that other people are enjoying—a world you are not seeing for yourself. You must look at the future and not just at the day-to-day circumstances. It is like driving a car on the highway when the steering goes out. You know immediately you are in trouble and heading for the ditch. When it comes to one's financial future, most people are heading for the ditch. But without the strong feeling of shock caused by loss of control it seems so far in the future they put off doing anything about it.

Here is your opportunity to check your knowledge level and the actions you are taking concerning your personal financial management style.

The following is a self-assessment tool that can help you determine whether or not you are on track financially. You may find that you want to expand your knowledge and acquire the tools that take you from whatever life style/level you are in to a higher, more pleasant and successful level.

Please take the test and see what you know. It is important to be totally honest with yourself. If you don't know all the answers it means you are a typical American. It also indicates you should change what you are doing.

Financial Health Checkup

1. Do you have at least 10 percent of your income going into savings or investing every month? Yes _____ No _____

2. What is your current net worth? $ _____

3. Of your net worth how much is in appreciating assets? $ _____

4. Do you know how to calculate the amount of unearned income you will need when you retire and enjoy a comfortable life? Yes _____ No _____

5. Do you worry about your current money needs or that you won't have enough income to live on when you retire? Yes _____ No _____

6. Are you working on a plan to get completely out of debt including your home mortgage in seven to nine years? Yes _____ No _____

7. How much money do you need to set aside each month to cover your wants and needs for the next twelve months? $ _____

8. What is your credit report mid score? _____

9. Do you know how to read your credit report? Yes _____ No _____

10. Have you ever been able to raise your credit score? Yes _____ No _____

11. How much cash will you have at the end of each month for the next three months after you have paid your debts and expenses? $ _____

12. How many investment opportunities have you looked at in the past week? (0) (1–5) (6–10)

Through 25-plus years of helping people with financial management I have found few participants can accurately answer the previous questions. After our workshops the students know how to calculate and use the tools to produce accurate and timely answers.

This self-check may be an eye-opener. I hope so! You may find out what you should know in order to be financially healthy. If you don't know the answers it should serve as a wake-up call. If you don't intervene you may be heading for a disastrous financial future, living a life of poverty. That leads us to Mission Number Two.

Mission Two—To have this book become a wake-up call, especially for those who are surviving today, but not taking action to prevent financial disaster.

Your test results should show you what you need to know and create enough discomfort to make you want to keep reading. It should also convince you who are living a healthy lifestyle to want more, even if only to protect what you have. You need to see that you are not reaching your full financial potential. The problem is that we are creatures of habit and like to stay in our comfort zone, even if it is not good for us and holding us back from being really comfortable in the future.

To have this effect you will have to experience fear for your financial future, or become frustrated with not having enough money to live on. It may catch your attention if you have had enough stress and are willing to make changes. It will work for you if you really want the pleasure of a wealthy lifestyle. Maybe you will get angry about having others control your money. Whatever your current attitude, I hope it will give you the drive and energy to change your life. If not, the lack of inertia will keep you financially trapped.

If high income earners are also high consumption people who buy depreciating assets, they will still be living paycheck to paycheck. If low income earners have learned the skills and want to control their finances they can become financially healthy without a large increase in pay. The opportunity for abundance is in your grasp if you are willing to put in the effort to move to a higher level of financial lifestyle.

This book is about intervention. It means drastic change must take place if you want to alter your financial lifestyle. This book is for you if you are not happy financially or have fear for your future. The feeling must be influencing enough for you to do what it takes to be in charge. It is also my attempt to bring back America's middle class—one person at a time. Eventually, it could help America to once again become economically healthy.

Mission Three—To give those who wish to take charge and improve their financial lives a way to get started quickly.

You will see the entire picture along with the step-by-step process needed to become financially healthy and even beyond. To change financial behavior you must first commit to change. You will learn how to take charge of your finances. This will be explained in detail later on. The rewards will be so great that even when things go wrong financially, you will be able to quickly adjust.

It won't happen naturally. It takes time, learned lessons, and effort. The good news is that anyone can grow financially if they are willing to change. It doesn't matter what level of income or formal education you are starting from.

Most people don't like to deal with their finances because:

1. They like to assume they are getting along just fine.
2. It takes time, involves details, and that isn't much fun.
3. They don't know how to manage their personal finances
4. They don't want to deal with the true picture.
5. They wouldn't know what to do even if they knew where they stood.

It may come as a surprise, but the level reached in formal education or the amount of income doesn't necessarily affect which level of financial lifestyle a person is living. For many reasons, it is much harder today to move to a higher lifestyle than in the past. There is less income growth potential, and much more opportunity than ever in our history for money going out.

Mission Four—To give to those willing to take the time and make the effort to become healthy or wealthy the total information they need, presented in sequence. This makes it easy to learn the necessary lessons, the tools to practice with, the actions to take, the challenges to overcome, and the rewards to achieve to reach their goals.

You need to learn the entire sequential process. The developmental actions must be taken when the timing and your financial knowledge and capabilities are right. No matter what lifestyle you are in you will need to use the tools and take the prescribed actions to reach the next higher level. You can't skip the lessons because they will give you a new mind-set or focus from which to look at your changing new world. Otherwise it would be like going to a 3-D movie without the glasses—it would only be blurry. By following this process you will enjoy a successful journey. Therefore, you won't fail or quit. It will be important to take the needed action and do what matters. This book will help you do that.

Mission Five—To help keep the pride in America. One person at a time intervening to become healthy financially will help alter the path that our middle class is on. We are the richest and most powerful nation in the world, but we are on a path to financial self-destruction. We will have a society of very few "haves" while the masses will be "have-nots".

Use this as your guide. It will coach you through the challenges, provide you with the new information you need, give you the tools to use, and help you make the mind-set adjustments. It will take you one step at a time and prepare you for the next higher level of financial lifestyle. As soon as you reach another level it will give you the c hallenges, needed lessons and actions to take to again move to the level beyond the one you just reached.

Mission Six—To have you enjoy and use this book to its fullest potential for you. I hope you will enjoy reading this book. More important, I hope you use it as a guide to become financially successful.

The missions of this book are to help all of you who are not living financially peaceful and want successful life changing strategies and systems. My mission is to help anyone who is willing to intervene in their life, learn the steps and use the tools to be highly successful in producing a wonderful financial life. By helping as many people as this book can, we will bring back and stabilize the middle class in America. It is a huge dream, but every journey starts with one step or, in this case, one person.

Chapter **TWO**

Why Read and Use This Book?

It is my goal to share the knowledge I have learned with anyone who cares about their finances. The path to working your way to financial health and beyond is to take a systematic linear approach. This is not a get-rich program, but a means to become wealthy starting with your current income. You will need to see the world differently, from a financial perspective, and take different actions, forming new habits. If you stay focused and follow the systems presented in this book you will be able to navigate with ease, taking one correct important step at a time.

If you follow the information provided here you will create all the money you need to live comfortably the rest of your life. During your journey you will take control of your spending, get out of debt quickly, create good credit, learn the lessons, and assimilate the behaviors of the wealthy. You will become wealthy. At this point, because you have gained the education and formed the right habits, you will never fear regressing or losing what you have gained. With intervention through education you will be able to duplicate becoming wealthy anytime you need. Becoming wealthy is a set of learned behaviors. Once you learn the process you will own it forever.

Without changing the way we operate financially, it is my belief that the American middle class will soon be in deep trouble. This knowledge is backed up by the information the media frequently report. It indicates the trouble the American middle class is heading for—if not already there.

People fail to change because they don't know how or it's too easy and comfortable to stay the course. To be successful, passion and commitment must be fueled until the person not only gets to practice new behaviors and insights but reaps the benefits of the rewards. The rewards will reinforce the use of the new behaviors as they become habits.

One of the strongest points made for each of the five financial lifestyles comes in the challenge portion. This represents the roadblocks you must overcome to reach the next higher level of financial management growth.

After reading this book you will know the challenges you will face on each level. This will give you a heads-up to what you need to do to keep moving forward. Your progress will be thwarted if you only get the knowledge without implementing the behaviors or getting past the challenges.

Intervention is needed to stop what you are doing and implement new behaviors. You can develop through each level of lifestyle until you reach the one where you want to live. In order to do this you must follow, in sequence, the entire process. If you don't maintain your belief and commitment while taking this journey, the setbacks and discomfort for doing something new will pressure you to quit. If you do not commit you will most likely regress to an earlier level of behavior. Support in your efforts is important. It helps to get a spouse, significant other, friend or a new support group to take the journey with you. You can make it—don't give up!

The new focus and skill set you learn will have to be practiced until they are "owned"—they become automatic. This is true for what you focus on, how you think, and what you do.

Another major observation I have made is that people live a certain financial lifestyle—one of five, to be exact. They are not trapped in a lifestyle but, without education, the tools, and the right actions, change doesn't happen. They are imprisoned by the way they think and the way they act. They know other people are better-off financially but they themselves don't know how to change.

Controlling your money and operating from a budget are more difficult than in past years. There are so many new items to own, and, with two adults both working, we look for convenient services and products. One of the first keys to success is to understand and implement a "needs" not a "wants" buying strategy.

We are losing the war on financial health. You can help by first helping yourself and passing it forward to help others become financially healthy and wealthy.

Chapter **THREE**

The Extinction of the Middle Class in America

In my 25-plus years teaching personal financial management for different organizations I have gained much knowledge that I want to share. I have had phenomenal experiences as a high school teacher and counselor, business owner and trainer, and business broker and marketer of real estate to investors. My education comes from working with people from all levels of income and financial success. I have taught blue-collar workers making minimum wages to highly paid business owners and successful entrepreneurs. From these experiences I understand why some people become wealthy and others stay stuck and merely get by.

Today's middle and lower classes are on autopilot, heading for financial disaster. If they don't decide to take charge and change their course they will retire poor. I have also worked with people going through bankruptcy and those who have lost their homes to foreclosure. Our company holds a class almost every week for the folks going bankrupt. These clients often make the comment after our workshops, "I wish I would have had this class years ago." I wonder: If they had taken the training would they still be going through bankruptcy? I think I know the answer. The federal bankruptcy laws require anyone going through bankruptcy to take two courses. The one we teach is the second. Maybe there should be a law that requires this course before people can get a loan. My education prejudice is showing. I believe in preventive teaching. I know if the bankrupt folks would have had the training and taken the actions prescribed in this book, most would not be going through bankruptcy and probably could be wealthy.

The real indications that the middle class is becoming extinct are found in the following: Americans aren't saving any money and are living paycheck to paycheck. According to an article in *The Wall Street Journal*, 70 percent of Americans are living one paycheck away from trouble. A recent Associated Press article and a major newscaster reported that the American savings rate this past year was worse than it has been for 74 years. It now matches the rate of savings during the Great Depression. It is a negative number. We are now burning into what little savings we did have. The general population is spending more than it is earning. Most retirees in this country are living on Social Security alone. We are experiencing the highest home foreclosure rate ever. There are more than a million personal bankruptcies per year in this country. The debt owed to other countries is the highest it has ever been. The consumer debt level is huge. We are now being enticed by retailers to buy merchandise and not make payments for up to four years or more, in addition to the amount of money paid every month by those debtors who are not paying on time, therefore paying higher interest, late fees, and penalties.

I have just read a national news article claiming that some of the credit card companies are targeting recently bankrupt people and providing them with credit cards, hoping they fill up their new credit limit and will fail to pay on time. This will generate huge returns in late fees and penalties to the credit card companies. When this is added to the high interest rate, the credit card companies gain enormous returns. The "cash for your future paycheck" stores are popping up all over. Tax returns with immediate refunds for a discount are frequently used by those who need cash instantly.

Another sign of the times is the advent and promotion of the reverse mortgage. Those who lived at the level they could afford and paid off their homes are now refinancing and pulling money out for monthly living expenses. It isn't only a reverse mortgage; it's a reverse move financially. It will help some people survive but will hurt others and their heirs.

The divorce rate, which has been high for years is said to often be caused by money problems. These are the overt symptoms.

All these facts bother me greatly. How can we live in the richest, most powerful country in the world and be heading toward 70 percent of our citizens living in poverty? This doesn't bode well for my pride as an American. What are we thinking? Now is the time to change. You have a decision to make: Are you going to become a have? Or a have-not? We are heading for a two-strata economic and social system— the wealthy and the poor.

Our schools are not addressing the issue. We don't teach people how to become and stay financially healthy. There are books, CDs, home-study courses, and radio shows on personal finance. We can turn this situation around, but it has to be done one person at a time. This book will, if you desire, teach you how to change, give you the total picture. Our company offers ongoing training and support that helps you succeed faster. Visit *www.creatingmoneyforlife.com.*

Causes of the Cash-Poor and Low-Net-Worth Middle Class

The creation of credit cards, the growth of large banks and finance companies, along with liberal lending policies, have greatly affected individual financial lifestyles. Most families, after the Great Depression, lived a healthy lifestyle. Once it became easy to borrow money for anything you wanted, however, financial health started to erode. The advent of credit cards spawned impulse and immediate gratification buying. It is our own fault as consumers to keep that trend growing. However, the magnitude and constant bombardment of advertising keeps us from deviating from those behaviors. Interest payments are the death of most middle-class financial futures. People in days past couldn't buy unless they had the cash. Therefore, they were forced to plan, be patient, and live within their means. Now you can live off tomorrow's paycheck. Back in the old days it only took one partner working to be solvent. Now because of debt, impulse buying and the number of items to buy, people are living broke, even with two working adults. The credit availability has greatly changed our mind- sets. We want it now and will worry about paying for it later. Immediate gratification and impulse buying are habits most of us have. Personal bankruptcy and home foreclosures used to be a rarity and very emotional. Now it seems to be a financial strategy.

Income growth is slowed by many factors. There are fewer

large manufacturing companies that offer promotion from one level to a higher level every few years. Those companies no longer exist or they have merged and been gobbled up by huge corporations. These huge corporations have flattened their management levels. They have also utilized robots, technology, and foreign labor to replace employees. Therefore, fewer career moves are in the offing. There are fewer companies in any one industry and the diversity of technology creates less opportunity. Therefore, one cannot go to a competitor and get a large raise for doing a similar job to the one just left.

The cost of health insurance is taking a big bite out of wage and salary increases. Social Security funding is now year-round for most people and the wage earner doesn't get the extra 7.65 percent midway through the year. In addition, employers pay the 7.65 percent all year and have less money for raises.

We as American consumers are also to blame because we want to buy goods at a discount. The fast growth of discount stores is a product of our buying habits. It has caused lower profits for the manufacturing companies, which means less money for raises. It also means more jobs are being transferred to foreign countries.

The mass growth of entrepreneur-owned small companies is now the mainstay of our economy. Small companies just don't have enough profit to offer much in raises. The same holds true for school systems and municipalities.

The amount of money an individual needs to survive in the style to which we are all accustomed has greatly increased in the past few years. Technology, with its magnificent advantages, is also causing financial hardships. But don't blame technology; it is our impulse buying and immediate gratification that causes the real problem. We want every new gadget, we also want every upgrade, and we want it now.

Another aspect is that we are getting trapped into ongoing monthly expenses. A new way for companies to create ongoing income and keep customers paying month after month is to lock them into an agreement. Rental offers on cars haven't been around for very many years. We also have movie rentals with a monthly fee. Rent-to-own stores are all over to "help" the disadvantaged—those people who have no cash and poor credit. What is the true cost of the appliance or furniture compared to what the cash-poor would pay if they had some money and good credit? We are no longer a "buy it, take care of it, and keep it for years" society. We are a "buy it, upgrade it, throw it away, and buy more" society. We also no longer take the "buy it with cash and only pay for it once" approach.

A new style of monthly fee has come into effect. You are charged for being hooked up even if you don't use the service that month. We now have a monthly bill for cable TV instead of an antenna. Even though we can enjoy hundreds of channels it is no longer free (at $50 to $125 per month). We are hooked into the Internet and we have to have high speed, which is another monthly bill. Instead of a landline $9 a month phone bill, everyone in the family has a cell phone at $50 to $100 per month. These are in addition to the monthly fees and taxes we must pay for services each and every month.

We are now experiencing the day of taxes and fees. *Money* magazine recently had an article stating fees for banking and credit were only one third of what they were just five years ago. Water bills are no longer based on usage but on being hooked up. My recent landline phone bill was for $14.98. After adding the federal and state taxes and access fees, the total payment was $26.45—an increase of 45 percent. If you want to get irritated, start reviewing all bills to see what you are actually paying for the service. Because we throw away new technology every two or three years, the marketing strategies are to get us hooked and have us "need" upgrades. In addition, service companies have learned that a great way to ensure future sales is to charge a monthly fee.

Inflation, even at 2 or 4 percent, when compared to the low raises most Americans are receiving each year, reduces buying power. It also means no extra money for savings or investing. The national formula for calculating the consumer price index and predicting inflation rates doesn't consider raises on taxes, fee increases in phone bills, electric bills, heat bills, cable bills, refuse bills, water and sewer bills, and on and on. Everything we buy and do seems to have creeping increases. We are suffering from the squeeze. A possible exception is clothing, which is made more cheaply in foreign countries, thanks to lower labor costs and foreign government financial support. It is nice to save $10 on a shirt, but if you don't have a job it doesn't matter.

Many service contractors offer good, up-front deals. The loss leader concept gets you in for only $33 a month, but two years from now you will be paying $100 a month. Lost leader marketing strategy is to offer low cost on an item to get you to buy. In the case of retail store it gets you in and you buy additional items. For the service sector, it is a low sign up fee to get you to change to them. They will soon raise the fee or rate. The selling strategy is to get you hooked up and continue to bill you every month, in addition to the rate frequently increasing the rate. Credit card companies, using the same strategy, are mailing many offers per week to those who have reasonably good credit.

Municipalities used to charge us for water and sewer use. Now they charge a fee even if you didn't use any, just for having the service hooked up. I own a rental house that is vacant. The water bill for the last three months was for $30; the bill reflected zero usage. No one was living there. I found out when I called the city that just being hooked up cost $10 a month, even if the water was shut off at the incoming valve.

With the computer come frequent upgrades, ink and paper, new software, exposure to buying on the Internet, and, every few years, new hardware—not to mention downtime when installing, learning to use it, or problems caused by the new upgrades. Energy costs are taking a $100 monthly bite out of the budget. Heating bills and travel have jumped in cost.

There are many changes in the way we buy homes. Not so long ago you couldn't get a zero-down mortgage or roll your closing costs and prepaid expenses into the mortgage. This is now prevalent. It indicates that people don't have any money to put down. It also shows that people are signing up to pay a lot more interest. Another sign in the housing industry is the huge number of people who refinance their houses every two to three years and pull out the equity to pay off debts. Then, they fill up their credit limits and refinance in two or three years once again. You can't become debt-free doing that. Going into retirement and making house payments can be a large burden. If your home is free and clear you could get a reverse mortgage and pull money out without making payments on it if needed. But if you keep burning up your equity that option won't be available.

Taxes have increased. Look at your phone, electric, heat or cable bill and see the amount of federal and state taxes. These increase your monthly costs, therefore reducing company profits.

One of the largest hits on our money is credit. Before credit cards we had to plan ahead, be patient, and pay cash for most items. Now we spend more. According to retail statistics consumers spend about 40 percent more in stores that offer credit. But the real problem is not paying the balance off at the end of each month. There exists trillions of dollars of consumer debt. Those monthly charges can cripple personal finances. The people living in the prosperity or wealth lifestyle only pay interest on appreciating and passive-income producing assets. Meanwhile the healthy-, control-, and survival-level people are wasting money and future gain on debt interest.

Chapter FOUR

Who Controls Your Money?

The following is a list in order of influence. These influences affect everyone. However, they effect people differently. For those who manage their finances and have taken control they have much less effect than those who allow these influences to be in control. The individuals living the higher level lifestyles have learned to get rid of debt, do tax planning to lower their tax burden, and avoid buying from impulse reaction or immediate gratification. Therefore, they are in control and have more discretionay dollars to save and invest. The order is one through seven, one being the strongest impact and seven being the least. Until someone intervenes and takes control, most people are in the No. 7 position. Most people start in that position, and, as they become more aware and in financial control, they change the order. That order indicates who or what entity controls your money. First, the taxes are taken before you get your net or take-home pay.

Even when people think they are in the No. 1 position, the

actual hierarchy looks like this for those lving in the lower level lifestyles:

1. Taxes
2. Debts
3. Expenses
4. Advertising
5. Salespeople
6. Cash, savings account, or check balance (your ego)
7. You—your logical self comes last

People living at the survival level don't usually pay any attention to income taxes except when they have a refund coming. I often ask class participants in the first quarter of the year how they did on their taxes. Most say "great" because they are getting $1,000–$3,000 back. I next ask: How much did you pay in? Most don't have a clue; they never looked at their gross income—only what they bring home. The important aspect is not how much you make but how much you get to keep. Did you know that when you get a tax refund it means you gave the government an interest-free loan? You paid in more than you had to!

When people get into the healthy lifestyle, they start to organize their debts, expenses, income, deductions, and investments to take advantage of the legal ways to pay less taxes. People living the prosperous lifestyle have hired professional accountants, tax planners, and attorneys to help protect their earned income and assets. They have goals of creating more passive income and taking advantage of tax deductions, shelters, and credits.

As people move to the control lifestyle they get a handle on the money going out and start to make adjustments. Healthy-lifestyle people spend by a plan, track their money, find ways to cut the expenses, and are interested in having savings. They begin to focus on the seven influences.

Taxes

Federal, state, and local municipalities take income tax off the top. They come first. People living at the survival or control levels don't do anything to take advantage of altering their deductions or looking at other tax-saving opportunities. Once people reach the healthy level they become more upset with the amount they pay out. Those living the prosperity and wealthy lifestyles do what they legally can to pay much less. The amount you pay is based on what you know and how you manage your money. Survival-level people don't do anything about lowering their taxes. Wealthy people spend a lot of time finding ways to legally avoid paying any more tax than necessary.

Debts

Debts are the monies you pay out to cover the cost of borrowing. You either borrow directly (meaning you got the money) or you borrow indirectly (meaning you bought and charged a car, a home, other items or services and didn't touch the money). The money transfers from the lender to the supplier. Once you sign the papers you are liable for the payments until the loan is paid in full. I like to say you are stuck with the payments. It gives a more true meaning.

Survival-level persons have created debt to buy depreciating assets such as clothes, TVs, cars, refrigerators, and so forth. Healthy-lifestyle participants save and pay cash for those items. Prosperous-lifestyle participants sometimes borrow to invest in appreciating assets and those that create passive income—such as buying a business. The business venture would create earned income.

The problem with depreciating assets and expenses paid with debt is that it is committing use of future income. Not only is the debt for interest, it is also taking money that could be saved for future wants and needs. Paying cash for the products or services can save hundreds of thousands of dollars over a lifetime. People making $20 per hour for 40 hours a week in a normal working lifetime will earn more than $1.5 million. The key to wealth is making sure you do the right thing with the money and avoid using it to pay debt. If you use it to buy appreciating assets and passive income-producing assets it will make you wealthy and help you create money for life.

Buying a car is a good example. Cars today will last for at least 10 years. If people would keep them that long it could change their finances. A good strategy would be to buy a one- or two-year-old used car and finance it for as short a time as you can afford.

Worst case—you finance it over five years. Why not pay it off in five years and for the next five years, put your payment aside, and then use it as a down payment for your next car? The problem is that survival-level people buy expensive cars that have too many miles on them and won't last ten years. In a few years the car needs repairs and they trade it in early and turn the loan-to-value ratio upside down and get deeper in debt. So they get trapped paying interest for their entire life. How many thousands of dollars do they pay in interest? That money could have been saved for emergencies or invested for their future income.

The people living the prosperity and wealthy lifestyles don't take on debt unless it is for acquiring appreciating assets.

Expenses

The next money control is your expenses. There are fixed expenses, those which have a similar payment each month, such as rent or an insurance premium. There are also variable expenses that change each month, such as heat, electricity, clothing, and groceries.

Survival-level people don't take control of their expenses; therefore, they function in an out-of-control manner. They continue to spend their money through impulse and immediate gratification. They fail to work diligently on controlling or cutting their expenses. Through our classes I have yet to see anyone who couldn't make 5 percent to 10 percent average cuts on their variable expenses. The only ones who can't are the ones who don't think they can or just plain don't want to.

People are often living beyond their means because they make buying decisions based on whether they think they can handle the monthly payment, not on wants versus needs or how the purchase fits with any kind of plan. We meet with prospective lease-option clients each week who will go through the application and approval process, but, until the day they sign the papers, have never asked the price of the house. Much earlier in the process they did ask what the monthly payment was.

Our survival-level clients have high car payments, high cell-phone bills, high cable television bills, and so forth. Many don't honestly feel they can cut or do without. Becoming financially healthy isn't that important to some. They don't feel the fear of what will happen to them in their later years. Being on a slight financial diet when you are in the survival, control, and health modes will get you to the prosperity and wealth mode, at which time you will have all the money you need for the rest of your life and can buy what you want. But many don't know another lifestyle exists for them. They lack the confidence, the drive, and the belief they can and deserve to change, or have the knowledge and tools to change their behavior.

Advertising

Advertising controls money as it creates interest and helps people move to a desire to own. The average person gets hit thousands of times a day with flyers, newspapers, catalogs, radio, television, posters and mail ads each day. The purpose for the millions of dollars spent is to get your attention. The credit card companies spent over 9 billion, yes with a b, dollars last year on advertising that helps continue the immediate gratification and impulse buying behaviors. It gets an emotional reaction from those who, in some cases, don't even know they are interested in what the ad is selling. But for someone who is on the borderline of want, it will force them to take action. If you want a simple test: For 30 days avoid listening to or reading any advertisements. See the money you will save. The highest per-square-foot sales area of a retail store is the hanging Peg-Boards lining the checkout counter. As you stand and read the information it's easy to grab items and add them to your shopping cart. Was it really something you needed? Was it on your list? Most likely not!

Salespeople

The salesperson's job is to get you to buy, get you to upgrade and spend more, get you to buy a more expensive model, get you to buy more items, get you sign up for maintenance or service contracts, get you to open a credit account, and get you to come back soon to buy more often.

They often have had many hours of sales training. How many hours of consumer protection training have you had? Most of us have had none.

Cash on Hand and in Your Checkbook

This controls your money by being a false sense of having extra money. Most people haven't established a set-aside account and therefore don't know how much money they need to keep in reserve—to have all the money they need for the next year. So they operate within what I call a sick-stomach sense of decision making. This means that most people have a level of money in their cash drawer or checkbook that represents a threshold point. If they get under that amount they become uncomfortable and begin to worry or experience anxiety. That amount is individually based. For some people it is $300; for another it could be $2,000. It depends, somewhat, on income.

The problem is, if there is a balance over their threshold, they have a tendency to believe they are in a good position and will often buy from those funds. In reality, if they had a set-aside account and used the defense mechanism of having their money harder to get to, they would know the money is allocated to paying something in the future. Therefore, they would be less likely to spend it. Once it is gone, it is gone. When the future bill comes due that requires the reserve, they have to get it from somewhere.

The Cycle of Negative Cash Flow and Heading for the Ditch Goes On

Those who spend money without a plan can never afford a vacation unless they charge it. If they want to go to Hawaii for two weeks they can never go without a plan. If they put $45 a month into their set-aside account for five years they would have $2,700. But if they continue to blow $45 a month on yard sales and other stuff, they will never go.

What if they invested the $45 a month at 8 percent for 20 years? They would have $26,505 toward a retirement. And if they added the money they pay every month on debt, say $1,000, and added an extra $350 for a new income-producing idea, what would they have after 10 years? The answer is $255,209. At a 6 percent return without touching their principal they would have created income of $1,276 a month for life. Creating passive income streams is the basis for creating money for life.

You

If you are living at the survival level you are in seventh position for being in control. Taxes, debts, expenses, advertising, salespersons, and cash in your checkbook all come before you. Even though most people feel they are in control, they are not. If they were, they would all be wealthy.

Those living in the control level are in fifth position. They move ahead of cash in checkbook and expenses. They still need to progress above advertising and salespeople. Those living the healthy lifestyle are in third position. They are still controlled by taxes and debts. Those living in the prosperity lifestyle are in second position. Only taxes control them when it comes to handling their money. Those who reach the wealth lifestyle are No. 1. They are actively controlling their taxes as much as possible. They pay what is legally due. However, they take advantage of tax-deferred and tax-free IRAs, 401(k)s, and other write-off investments, such as real estate.

The last influence on controlling most people's money is themselves. If they take charge and intervene in their spending, work from plans and use the right systems, they can alter their own financial future—to be the best they want to be.

Who will control your money starting today? Hopefully you! Think about it, stay focused on it, and start to intervene. It is your money. Why not become wealthy now instead of letting others control your money, which will cripple your wealth-building future? You just need to get off autopilot and change your spending habits. Get out of your comfort zone and intervene in your complacency. You will be blessed for doing it.

Chapter FIVE

The Five Financial Lifestyles

There are five financial lifestyles. People can choose which one they want to live in. My experience shows that neither level of income nor level of formal education has a strong correlation with the lifestyle people live. You were raised in a certain lifestyle and imitate that, or you changed. Those who were raised in a higher lifestyle and regressed fell into their wants personality and formed bad habits. Those who moved to a lifestyle higher than that in which they were raised wanted more and learned new behaviors from their parent's example.

This book will explain the differences among the five lifestyles. It will provide the ways to develop to a higher level. This will be done by giving the challenges, the rewards, the lessons needed to learn, and the actions to take to progress through the lifestyles. Without the total understanding that this book provides one will most likely fail to grow to their potential.

Often lottery winners, highly paid professional athletes and actors end up broke. They live at the lowest level. This proves that the income level or even a huge signing bonus or millions won in the lottery don't provide the education to form the habits needed to change one's life. These high-income people who have a high-consumption survival-level style will remain in that mind-set even when given large sums of money.

I have had low-income clients do extremely well financially. Most of the wealthy people I know didn't inherit their money or win it—they put in the effort to get the right education. This often came from street-smart experiences and the right attitudes. It took them years to grow from one level to the next. In this book you will find the shortcut to wealth. Instead of learning by costly trial and error you can follow the steps and get through the maze of financial training much faster.

Financial Lifestyles

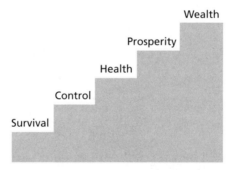

It is interesting to note why people are living the lifestyle they are in.

Here is a Quick Test to See What Level You are On

Answer to the best of your knowledge. Be honest—this is for your benefit only.

1. How much time did you spend this month randomly shopping in a mall, in stores, in yard sales? 0–2 hours, 3–8 hours, 8 or more.

2. How much time did you spend this past month reading about, researching or looking at investment opportunities? 0–2 hours, 3–8 hours, 9 or more hours.

3. How much time did you think or worry about not having enough money to pay bills or not having enough to retire on? 0–2 hours, 3–8 hours, 9 or more?

4. How much money did you put this past month in your IRA, 401(k), stocks, bonds, mutual funds, or other investments? 0–$100, $100–$3,000, $3,001 or more?

5. If you needed or wanted to increase your income, how would you do it?

   a. By working overtime or taking on another job

   b. By cutting expenses

   c. By investing in a vehicle that will bring in more income

   d. By creating a new marketing letter or promotion to your group of followers who you have built a product and services provider/buyer relationship.

6. Define the difference between appreciating assets and depreciating assets.

7. How much money did you spend this past month buying depreciating assets that you wanted, not needed? $0–$100, $101–$500, $501 or more.

8. How much time did you spend on planning, tracking, and reviewing the results of your finances this past month?

    a. 0–2 hours

    b. 3–5 hours

    c. 6 hours or more

9. How many different goals do you have written down for your financial growth?

    a. 0 to 2

    b. 3–5

    c. More than 5

10. How many hours did you spend this past month on tax planning?

    a. 0–2

    b. 3–5

    c. More than 5

11. If you won $100,000, what would you do with the money?

    a. Pay bills to catch up

    b. Buy a new car and use it for a down payment on a home

    c. Pay off debts and take a vacation

    d. Invest the money

Your answers will give you an idea about the lifestyle level you are living, along with your mind-set. Where are you spending your financial time and what are your current behaviors? If you want to advance, read further.

People living at the survival and control levels are spending time shopping and worrying about money. Those living in the healthy level spend time planning, goal-setting, and saving. Those in the prosperity and wealth levels spend time investing and protecting assets against loss and taxes. Those in the survival/control level think their only resource for increasing income is to work more. Those in prosperity and wealth invest or sell more to create income.

Where do you place yourself?

Mark an X on the continuum where you feel you are today and then mark an X where you want to be five years from now. See any difference? Next mark an X where you will want to be when you retire. If you feel anxious or unknowing—that's good. Now is the time to start intervening and creating your own future.

By changing your focus, knowledge, time spent, and behavior, you can consistently move up the ladder of financial wellness.

How to Use this Book to Keep Developing Financially

The lifestyle people are living is up to them. High-income, high-consumption people have the same challenges as low-income, high-consumption people. Everyone can get to the next level. By using the processes in this book you will be able to grow through each level, one at a time, until you are wealthy. This isn't necessary if you find true happiness on a lower level. The only warning is: If you become complacent and your needs change when you are in your golden years, will you be financially where you want or need to be? If you build more than you need, and you should, share it. In order to do so you need the drive to get you there. The same basic steps have to be followed on each level in order to be successful.

To change levels of lifestyle and become healthy, prosperous or wealthy you must do the following: First, get yourself motivated for change. The energy must be strong enough to create the drive to sustain your growth. This book will provide you with the lessons you must learn, the actions you must take, the mind-set you must develop and the challenges you need to overcome in order to move from one level to the next.

The mind-set at each level will define what beliefs you need to develop. Values, defined as what is right and important, will have to be accepted as they change. Each level requires a new set of thought patterns, intense focus, and new behaviors, in addition to building your financial self-confidence and positive attitude. These alterations will give you the focus, thought patterns, comfort zones, motivation, and rewards to progress smoothly all the way to wealth. You will need to understand the new lessons in enough depth so you change your thoughts. You can't just memorize them or they won't work. Practice will bring about ownership of your new habits until they are used automatically.

Second, you must take on the actions needed to further develop your lifestyle. These are all provided in this book. The actions need to be practiced enough so they become habits.

Even though they will become habits, you need to stay focused on those habits with the mission and excitement for further growth. You must understand and face the challenges and roadblocks that will be in front of you at every level. You must not take the easy route or quit until you have gotten over the challenges. Third and finally, you need to create your reward list and enjoy your growth by recognizing and rewarding yourself for your progress. Progress will give you a strong sense of control and the euphoria will increase your passion.

You must understand and take on the challenges needed to overcome the roadblocks. You must learn the lessons needed to complete the activities to move forward. You can't wait until you are wealthy before you get pleasure and removal of pain. You need to acknowledge and celebrate your successes along the way.

For each level you must admit where you truly are. You must confirm the belief that you are worth the growth, that you have the power and will to put in the effort to change— that you will read this book to understand where your roadblocks and challenges will come from. Take the time and put in the effort to learn a new set of systems and tools. Get the support you need to keep going. Stay focused and committed. Reward yourself for reaching the benchmarks of growth.

In the survival level people waste their money, in the control level people watch their money, in health mode people save and pay off debt, in prosperity they invest to create passive income, and in the wealthy lifestyle they live financially free. The challenge here is to protect assets.

You must sacrifice in the first three lifestyles so you will prosper later—you must have patience, knowledge of how to change, and gather support to make the change. Along your journey you will develop new priorities and enjoy your

progress. When you see the big picture and the long-term ef-
fects you will easily be able to handle the short-term sacrifices.
Your finances are programmed by your attitudes, current
knowledge, and behaviors. They are learned behaviors and can
be changed by learning new behaviors. Fifteen percent of the
change will come from new knowledge and tools, and 85 percent will come from actions and practice. Age doesn't matter
and you can teach an old dog new tricks.

Understanding of net worth is needed to create future
income—your wealth is not measured by the possessions you
have. Wealth is about the passive income you have created. It
will allow you to go any time and any where, stay as long as
you like, and buy whatever you want. Many people measure
wealth by net worth. The true reason for building net worth is
for what income it can produce.

For those who are impulse and immediate gratification
buyers utilizing buying defense mechanisms can help. Make a
list of why you shouldn't buy the item or service. Look for dis-
likes.

What lifestyle does one have with an attic, basement, out-
door shed, garage full of stuff, thoughts about renting more
storage, and having no money to pay their bills? Net worth does
not include depreciating assets such as personal items, cars, and
so forth. These are decreasing your net worth each day.

In order to build passive income you will need to invest
and think differently about your money. People living in the
lower financial levels don't see how important passive income
is. Prosperous and wealthy people not only wait until they have
the money to buy, they only buy after they have invested. They
also have money which the lower level people continue to use
to pay on debt. This behavior continues for most of the lower
level people's lives. That difference alone can make you

wealthy. The prosperous and wealthy pay cash for their cars. The other three levels leverage and buy with little or no money down. The wealthy use their leverage when they buy real estate investments and other appreciating assets. The lower levels create debt that keeps them from investing. They could invest. But they make bad buying decisions. Their money is constantly leaking. They feel good about acquiring wanted stuff. I know of an investor who makes around $45,000 a year income from his job and can buy real estate with little or no money down. This person, who doesn't have other debt and has created high credit scores, now owns 10 houses and is heading for passive income upon retirement. How many families do you know that make $45,000 a year and are up to their wallet in debt? The difference is in their mind-set and knowing what to do.

For instance, how would you tell your children they could pay cash for their future cars? You ask how? Buy a good car and keep it for 10 years. After you have paid off the car in 60 months on a five-year amortization schedule, take the payment amount and put it in a separate account for the next five years. Take that money to use a down payment on the next car. After doing this twice, you should have enough money saved to start buying cars with cash. You will save thousands on interest.

It is my sincere hope that you will give a copy of this book to your children. It can drastically change their financial behavior, success, and provide them with a bright future.

High-Income and High-Spending = Stalled on Lifestyle Continuum

People aren't born with the genes of a spender or wealth builder. These are learned behaviors and are not heredity—they are environmental. Many people who develop the health lifestyle become complacent and never progress. They feel comfortable because they have a few extra dollars to save and put into their IRA, 401(k), and so forth. The problem is they aren't looking out far enough as to what lifestyle they will want or need when they stop working. They may have higher expenses than they think. If they live 20 to 30 years after they retire, they can be facing many changes. They will go through three or four cars, and the cost of energy, health care, and long-term care are unknowns. The wealthy have their assets continuing to produce increasing passive income so they will be covered for almost any inflationary trends. I had a student last week ask me a question I seldom get. We were calculating her future income needs. The gurus tell us to figure on 60 percent to 80 percent of your current income. Who knows what your expenses will be or how long you will live? Her question was: "What if I want to have a more expensive lifestyle than I have lived so far?" Great question. Instead of planning on living within reduced means, why not create wealth and live the lifestyle you want? Intervene and redirect your money and you can have whatever you want. Financial success comes from higher-level thinking skills along with the courage to do it. You will never be hurt by having more money than you will ever need!

Chapter **SIX**

The Total Picture and Sequence Learning

This book is different from many financial management writings in that it expresses the importance of financial education in a sequence of learning systems and behavioral changes. Most authors who write about personal financial management or wealth building only give you pieces of the picture and some of the tools you will need. First, they fail to represent the complexity of know-how to grow through each higher level of financial lifestyle and don't address the five lifestyles. It is as if they want you to only learn to get out of debt and live within your means. Instead, let's change your behavior so your means keep growing.

Second, some don't see the entire behavior change needed at each level to get to the top rung. You need to take all of the 80-plus actions to reach the top in the shortest time and in the most efficient and effective manner possible.

The lessons and life-changing techniques will be simple to

understand. Most of them you have heard of but never used. There are a few critical tools that I have never seen in any of the hundreds of books I have read on the subject. My process, however, is unique. It is a step-by-step fast-track total package.

One example is that everyone knows you need to do a budget. It's simple, but it's important to know not only why you are doing it, but how it is needed to fit in with the health level and beyond to the prosperity and wealth levels. No one ever became wealthy by implementing a budget, setting a few goals, getting out of debt, doing nothing else. You must see the entire picture or you get all fired up, go on a financial diet, and not know what to do next. People who learn lessons out of sequence or try to use tools before the proper timing will get frustrated and quit. An example is: Many people read about investing or quick wealth building but never succeed because they never get in full control of their finances. To be successful you will need to read this entire book and put into place all of the action steps provided here. By moving through all the lifestyles you will gain the knowledge and make the needed behavior changes to fully intervene. Most people read a book on getting rich quickly and don't get the total education to make the change complete. They are trying to run before they walk. Intervention takes learning and using the right steps at the right time and in the proper sequence. The behaviors have to be used long enough to become habits. At this point they will be cemented in your operating patterns and stay part of you. I call them "owned" at this point. Those who merely try a few behavior changes will usually fall on their face or run into the ditch.

This is a big reason total financial management and wealth building isn't taught in schools, even though an attempt at teaching the basics is needed. The timing for the individual isn't immediately relevant, and therefore can't be rewarding.

Because we are talking about learned behaviors, if the tools and lessons aren't immediately practiced they will not become the habits needed. Many of the concepts can be taught in a theoretical setting. However, to influence one's behavior change and to be reinforced for continuation, the concepts have to be practiced shortly after the exposure takes place. To only understand the needed change won't have an effect and most likely will be forgotten shortly. Why should one become wealthy? The main reason is to ward off potential financial problems later in life. Once you have decided to commit the energy to grow into a higher lifestyle it is easy to use the momentum to keep growing.

This book is different in that it relates the lessons to learn and the actions needed at each stage of development. The entire process must be learned in proper linear form to work to its potential. Yes, if you learn only part or a few tools or part of the sequence it will be better than nothing. But why not take advantage of the whole program? It will help you become totally successful and in a much shorter time.

Once you have learned and practiced all of the lessons you will see phenomenal results. The rewards gained from the results will give you the needed reinforcement to keep growing financially. You will also have a total understanding of the process and of the big picture so you won't fail. You may slip back from time to time but you won't regress far or for very long because you will have the knowledge to quickly get back up. By knowing what comes next in your learning path—the lessons, the actions to take, the challenges you will face—you will have developed the insights and the foundation to keep progressing. You will just have to keep supplying the motivation. If you are traveling across the country without a plan or map and you get slightly off course, you will quickly get lost.

With a plan and a picture of the entire trip, you will stay on track or get back on track with ease when you stray. To stay out of the financial ditch you must be aware of what you are doing. By reading this entire book and using it for reference along your journey you will be able to stay on track and reach your goals efficiently. It will become your road map and GPS (Global Positioning System).

Armed with the whole box of tools and a manual of how to use them, you will be able to make the behavior modifications. This is a living process—not merely a learning process. Most people want to jump to the get-wealthy stage first. However, by learning the lessons and getting the tools out of sequence before you are ready, means you won't have developed the foundation for fast growth and long-term stability. Therefore, the lessons will only be theoretical and not life changing if you learn how to calculate your debt elimination plan but haven't found the money in your budget to accelerate the stacking method pay downs. What good is it?

Self-made wealthy people often say it is the education of how to invest that counts. If they lose all their money tomorrow they can become wealthy again in a very short time because they know the process. They have formed the habits.

The old Chinese saying, "Give me a fish and I eat for a day, teach me to fish and I eat for a lifetime" is appropriate in this setting. I only hope the educator's adage of "When the student is ready the teacher will appear" fits for you at this time. This prophecy is accurate when it comes to financial management. There are hundreds of thousands of Americans who never become ready students. They will therefore never be able to intervene. They will stay stuck in their lifestyle. Are you a ready student? This book will be your teacher if you work with it. Our company can be your support if you want it. Visit *www.creatingmoneyforlife.com*.

Chapter **SEVEN**

The Survival Lifestyle

The characteristics of those living in the survival lifestyle

These people are living close to their means, usually spending more than they bring in. They are broke because of overspending and being out of sync with the timing of their income and payment due dates. They get behind and get hit by late fees and penalties. They have less than one paycheck in reserve. Their credit suffers from late payments and having more than 50 percent of debt when compared to the credit limit on lines of credit. Most have used every bit of available money they can borrow. Their credit limit is filled up and they have old debt on their credit report that they have stopped paying. Survival level is a state of mind and a set of behaviors that isn't necessarily related to low income. It is directly related to the way people spend and manage their money.

I have worked with people who were in the low-income bracket. That doesn't mean they have to live in the survival lifestyle. They are not stuck, but they must intervene if they want change. They are only trapped in the survival level if they don't take the steps to change. We also see high-income, high-consumption people living on this level. They are still living from paycheck to paycheck. However, they usually have more formal education so they don't have the tendency of blaming others for their financial problems. They know they can only experience change if they do something about their situation. Some of them will stay in the survival lifestyle for their entire lives. Others will want to move up to the health lifestyle. Examples are all around us of two families with similar education and income levels but with two different financial results. Take, for instance, two doctors making $150,000 a year. They start in the same position but end up with drastically different results. One becomes wealthy and the other stays in the survival level. One buys a moderate home, a nice used car and keeps it for 10 years. The other buys an expensive home and two new luxury cars, trades them in frequently, and fail to do any financial planning or investing. One will end up wealthy; the other will continue to struggle. Your income doesn't matter—you can still live beyond your means.

Money magazine recently had an article about a couple with an income of $150,000 and living beyond their means. They are living at the survival level. They are constantly robbing Peter to pay Paul. They have zero savings and very low net worth. The assets they have are of the depreciating kind— assets that will decrease in value—except perhaps their home. They buy and accumulate stuff without a plan or regard to the item's potential for gaining value in the future. They don't operate from a budget and they don't know how spending will negatively affect their future finances. Once they fill up their credit limits they continue to buy large items from retailers who offer zero payments for up to three years. They assume the money will be available when the total debt is due. Most don't make it and pay over 20 percent interest charged back to the time they signed the note with the retailer. Their financial position keeps getting worse.

I recently saw an ad for carpeting with no payments for four years. This sounds good to those who don't have money and fail to do any financial planning. The high-income survivors are living a dream of having money in the future. Buying on time with no down payment should scare the heck out of everyone. To the survivor, it is exciting—a way for them to continue to buy. The ramifications for this type of loan, in most cases, are death to future finances, in addition to hurting your credit while waiting for the bomb to hit. Most survivor-level buyers will take the position that they will pay the loan off before the deadline date. The truth is most won't. They will be facing an installment loan with the highest interest rate allowed. Plus, because of the no-payment plan they will probably be charged hundreds of dollars more than they would have if they had paid cash. They see it as an opportunity. I see it as a liability. The people living at survival level sometimes get their furniture or appliances from a rent-to-own store. They pay a weekly or monthly payment. They do this because they have no money and bad credit. The total they will pay for the items is many times what they would pay if they had cash or good credit.

When a problem occurs that requires cash, survival-level practitioners are in an emergency mode. If the car breaks down and it requires a few hundred dollars, they have to either find the money by taking it away from paying other expenses or they pay bills late. They just keep paying their bills late. When they pay debts late it negatively affects their credit score.

When they need to borrow for another car or for any other purpose they get punished, either by getting turned down for a loan, paying high up-front fees or high interest rates. They often roll bad debt into worse debt. They buy a car when they owe too much on their last car, the dealer gratuitously gives them a new loan with a high-level interest rate and a value worth less than what they owe. In the finance world this is called being upside down. This is a sign of being out of financial control. It also indicates bad decision making.

Survival-level people can never afford what they consider luxuries such as vacations. They waste money on convenience. They buy what they really don't need, and, in most cases, can't afford. They impulse-buy—especially around holidays because they go into an ego/need state. This state temporarily offsets their frustration with always being broke. Due to the way they impulsively buy, they waste their money. They buy when they have cash in their pocket without planning on that money being allocated and needed for bills in the future. Immediate gratification and not having money to keep things in good repair cause more financial destruction. They don't understand or have the willpower to buy only what they need. They buy what they want and when they want it, regardless of the effect it will have on their future finances.

Their purchasing decisions are based on the amount of the monthly payment. They don't do future planning and don't see the whole picture. The ones who are living in the danger zone frequently get collection calls and operate from the scream level. They function by paying the creditors who call the most frequently and yell the loudest. The consumer who is in arrears on their payment get frustrated and makes promises they can't keep.

These people feel the only way out is to work more and create more income. They believe there is no way to improve their financial situation without getting another job or a large wage increase. Many other influences control their financial lives. They constantly are in financial crises and seem to have a black cloud over their heads. They don't manage their money; their money controls them by managing their thoughts and behaviors.

When they receive extra money in the form of presents, bonuses, extra overtime or tax refunds, they use part of it to catch up and then blow the rest. They don't have any plan for getting out of the hole they are in, let alone getting ahead. They can't create the plan because they have never been exposed to the education of how to formulate a working plan.

The constant argument from those living the survival level in our workshops is "I don't have any money." The truth is there are always expenses or buying habits to alter to create a little extra cash. Many, due to the lack of control and constant stress, function from a point of anger or depression. When they are angry or depressed they make bad decisions. Many feel they don't deserve better or they never will be any better-off. Becoming wealthy is out of the question in their minds. They believe living the wealthy lifestyle is for those born into money or the lucky ones who win the lottery.

These consumers are consumption-oriented and enjoy looking for things to buy. They don't have money or the awareness to take advantage of moneymaking opportunities when presented. Investing is far from their thought processes. They are not open to looking for or taking advantage of potential gains. They look for quick fixes and get-rich quick schemes.

The Mind-Set of Those in Survival Level

To understand your finances you must be able to compare your lifestyle to others'. If you want to change you will need to understand the lifestyle you want and be willing to change your mind-set. This includes what you frequently think about, what worries you most, what motivates you, and how you handle stress.

Survival-level people spend much of their time worrying about collection-agent calls and being embarrassed and harassed for not having the money to pay bills on time. Their frame of reference is from one of lack. Psychologically they don't believe they are worthy of having more. They see a future of the same survival lifestyle for the rest of their lives. Working smarter and doing financial planning is not in their thought processes. They feel financial gains can be gotten only by winning the lottery or working harder by putting in a lot more hours.

If they won or inherited a large amount of money they would quickly burn through it. They are today-oriented in their spending habits. They are always under pressure from needing money. Even if they had a huge amount extra it would be consumed rapidly. They don't have a mental picture of the difference between needs and wants. They will continue to buy wants instead of holding out and saving for needs. They don't understand the difference between depreciating and appreciating assets. The items they buy are depreciating assets and often add to their debt load. They will buy for today and worry about not having enough money to live on tomorrow. They will buy items on sale whether they need them or not. Their ego is fed by thinking they got a good deal. They feel they got a good deal even if it isn't something they need or might use.

You read about people getting huge sums of money and within a short time they are broke. They waste the extra money and still live by purchasing depreciating stuff. They fail to think about saving money, paying down their debts or investing. Their style is to squander any extra income.

Survival-level mind-sets merely get by. If challenged to restructure their finances so they have reserves, they argue that they don't have any extra money to change. The truth is, if they intervened by taking charge and making minor adjustments, they could be moving to a better financial lifestyle and creating savings. They could begin to invest without a major income increase. Without the knowledge and tools for change it won't happen.

They never think about investing as a way to produce future unearned income. Many lottery winners and highly-paid athletes and actors often go broke because their thoughts and actions are in the survival lifestyle. If they would invest their gain and get the money creating more assets and income, they could become wealthy. Those who progress to a healthy, prosperous or wealthy lifestyle have to change their thought patterns. Those who succeed quickly upon receiving a large windfall of money take one of two paths: They put the money into savings until they go through the needed changes to alter their lifestyle, or they hire an advisor who directs their money for them.

These people feel they need every bit of income to pay bills. They often are willing to save or invest except they can't find even a few dollars for this purpose. They feel they are locked into their finances. They don't spend any time looking at their finances or their spending habits—they feel it wouldn't do any good. Therefore, they don't look for ways to cut expenses. They are not willing to take the time to look for "leaks" in their spending. They can't tell you where the extra money goes every month. They often waste money by listening to salespeople. They are sold what they shouldn't buy. They lack the sensitivity to know they will need that money for future bills. They waste money by frequently paying late fees and penalties. Their constant focus is on just getting by—never on improving.

Here is a good test. Ask someone you know how many expenses they have cut, how much debt did they pay off, how much money they have saved, or how many investments have they looked at in the past 90 days. If you get a blank stare like you are crazy, or the answer "none", you know you are talking to a survival level person. Ask your adult children. If they reply as above, give them a copy of this book.

Survival practitioners will fill up their credit cards and never pay them off. They don't worry about their credit until it causes them problems in getting more loans or getting turned down for a job or a place to live. Many experience a borrowing level beyond what they can pay and their ability to get further credit is cut off. At this point they pay a bill or two late and it trashes their credit rating. They panic and run all over town to get a car loan or refinance their home. They get turned down by the financial institutions offering fair interest rates and up-front fees. In our workshops these individuals tell us, sometimes arrogantly, that they qualified for a car loan. Therefore, they are under the false impression that they have good credit. When asked the interest rate they reply "24 percent." Their credit is bad and is costing them thousands of dollars and they don't even know it. What will they pay in interest and could they have put the money to better use? You know the answer.

When making a financial decision survivalists don't consider their total debt. Their buying decisions are based on whether or not they feel they can make the monthly payment. Since they are not operating from any plan they don't know what they can or cannot afford. They are buying on emotion without seeing the whole picture. We have people signing a lease and option on a $170,000 home without asking the price of the house. They asked up front what the payment is. We also have people in our program who tell us they can afford $950 a month for housing when they have $1,800 a month gross income. Many people in our country don't know how to do the math. They don't know their total financial situation. If this is you it's okay. I hope this didn't offend you to the point that you're becoming defensive and unable to admit you need to change. Admitting this represents your behaviors and you are on the right path to seek change. You will next need to get the education to intervene and become what you want financially.

In the real estate world we see everyday people who refinance their homes to pay off credit card debt and burn up their equity. Their house appreciates in value; however, they have filled up their credit cards again. So in a short time they refinance once more and their home is financed at or above market value. They are abusing one of the most important reasons to own a home.

The Rewards of Living the Survival Lifestyle

People living in the survival lifestyle have few, if any, rewards. Their only reward is that they can be complacent and truly block out their financial problems. However, most are surviving by constantly being under stress. Their reward comes from the emotional high from buying, which reinforces the habits of spending money as often as they get it.

Lessons to Learn While Living the Survival Lifestyle

The first lesson is for you to develop willpower based on the new belief that you deserve a better life. You must learn to say "no" or "not now" to purchases. You need to get comfortable walking away from buying situations. You must learn the difference between buying wants and buying needs.

The old adage "cash is king" must be felt by those living at the survival level because their actions keep them in the position of being a servant to the "kings" (banks and finance companies). Current TV ads for a credit card company states something like: a new dress $125.00, new shoes $80.00, wearing these to a family Thanksgiving dinner, priceless. For everything else there is credit cards. The answer in your future must be . . . for everything else there is savings. You need to learn to ask yourself: "What else do I need this money for in the future?" or "How can I better use this money to get ahead?" You must learn the damage that borrowing money is doing to your financial future.

Another important lesson is how you are being sold emotionally. This knowledge will help you stop being on autopilot when buying. We buy emotionally and without knowledge of what is happening to us. Millions of dollars are spent every year on training salespeople. No dollars are spent on consumer training teaching how to avoid buying.

You will need to learn to defend yourself against wasting money and buying what you don't need. You will need to know the difference between fixed and variable expenses, in addition to learning the difference between debts and expenses. You will need to learn what a set-aside account is and why it is important to have one.

Actions You will Need to Take to be Successful During the Survival Lifestyle

1. Start using alternative means of buying so you avoid using credit. Avoid creating any further debt. Stop borrowing money.

2. Stop reading advertisements.

3. Start keeping a list all of your expenses and debt payments.

4. Read about the proper use of credit and how debt affects one's freedom.

5. Stop charging anything unless it is an absolute emergency.

6. Practice questioning all purchases in respect to whether it is a true need or merely a want.

7. Tell yourself daily that some of your expenses can be reduced or cut out. Review your expenses to find those you can alter and list the dollars you will save.

8. Read and start using the buyer-defense mechanisms offered later in this book.

9. Review your debt against the debt warning signs found in a later chapter. See how close you are to being in trouble.

10. Take control of your finances. Stop spending money that is not already required for other more important purposes.

11. Start saving a few dollars each week.

12. Commit to paying all of your bills on time. Set up a system to keep track.

Information and Ideas to Help
You Take the Needed Actions

The AIDA formula is an acronym for a method taught to sales-people to find out how we emotionally get involved and quickly move from attention to buying.

Salespeople are trained to find our "hot buttons"—what gets us excited about their product or service. They talk features and sell the benefits. We like to think we are in control of the decision process when buying. The truth is we buy emotionally.

The first "A" in AIDA stands for attention. This can be done by advertising, retail displays, and all kinds of marketing techniques. Next we must get more emotional about the product or service—the "I" stands for interest. The third level of emotional intensity is the "D" that represents desire. And the fourth letter "A" stands for action. We will be given a directive as to how to buy.

You can understand the game we play by anticipating what the salesperson's next move will be and listening for manipulating information. Just say no! You can reverse the process by catching your emotional intensity between the interest and desire levels.

Defense Mechanisms for Not Buying

The first technique you should implement is to stop randomly shopping. Stay out of stores for 30 days, except for needed items such as gas for your car or groceries. Take this test for 30 days—you will be amazed how you save money.

It is also a good idea to avoid shopping on payday. On that day you feel better about your money, and, as explained earlier, have a false sense of extra money. Once you start paying bills your threshold of money will be closer and you will think more about not buying or buying less.

Another great technique is to avoid grocery shopping when you are hungry, only grocery shop from a list within your grocery budget. This, of course, takes some meal planning along with time and effort. This isn't as convenient, but it will help you become financially healthy. We ask this in class: "Where and on what do you spend your money?" Most people either don't know, or when their family size is compared to others' the amount of money is extremely diverse.

The use of coupons helps only if you buy items you will eat. Also, look for sales, which are frequent. Lower-shelved items are often cheaper than eye-level merchandise. Watch for generic products. If items are offering a rebate, take advantage if it is a good deal and you will commit to mailing in the rebate.

Control your spending. Until you reach the healthy level and beyond, you should be kept on a tight budget. Overspending can do much damage to your growth. You need to operate on a spending plan.

To avoid negative influences, stop reading and listening to advertisements. Only read about products when you have the budgeted money to pay cash and read the ads for research as to what and where to buy.

Set up an allowance for yourself. This is used for fun money. When you are in survival level you may only have $5 a week. As you grow toward the healthy level it can be a larger amount. This is not money for gas for your car or any expense you plan for. It is your play money. If you go on a financial diet, which most people will if they are serious about change, you will need an allowance. Otherwise it is like those who go on a food diet—for a while it works fine but if they are too restricted they fall off and binge eat. If you don't spend any money on yourself you will fall off and blow more than you can afford on stuff.

The rule with your allowance is that it has a cap. Whatever your budget dictates is your current limit. Your allowance will be an amount you can afford for the week. That amount is all you have. You can't have more until the next week, and no borrowing against future allowance.

The next defense technique is to set up your set-aside account. This is based on a prediction of monies needed to cover all debts, expenses, and savings for needs and wants for the next 12 months. This sounds tough, and it is at first. As you use it you will learn that it saves you in times of emergency and will help you have money to pay cash instead of charging or taking money needed for other expenses. Thus you end up paying late fees, penalties, and hurting your credit. It is a great planning tool for providing cash for luxury items or vacations. It is the tool that you will learn to use for adjusting your spending plan.

This is like a Christmas club for those who know they will spend $500 next December but won't have the money available unless they have a forced savings plan. At $41.66 a month × 12 = 499.92 (money they don't touch) would earn them $499.92 + interest for next Christmas. Why don't we do that with every large purchase, vacation, gifts, school expenses, home down payment, home repairs, and on and on? By using this secret weapon you can anticipate all future needs. It will shock you as you start to use it. We find that our clients have negative cash flow when they plot out all their needs, but enjoy the tool as it tells them exactly where they are and will be in the future.

Another wonderful technique is to use an envelope system

for paying bills either with actual envelopes or with a chart or computer to set money aside for next month's expenses. This is needed to be able to have the money available to pay all bills on time.

You should learn to use the "I am going to sleep on it" statement for protection—it works. This helps control one's emotions and is an important tool to stop buying on impulse or immediate gratification. Make a rule that on most purchases outside your spending plan you will take a 24-hour break to think about whether it is a want or need, to think about reasons not to buy, and to review your spending plan to find money to use if it is not in your current plan. What will you give up? This process will take the emotion and turn it to a logical process. Most of the time you will realize it isn't as important a buy as you felt at the time.

Watch for salespersons trained to handle your objections. They will try to give you more benefits or reasons why you need to buy now. Often this is done by short sales: "This price is only good until midnight." So what! You can probably find that product somewhere else cheaper, wait until it is out of season, wait until you have saved the cash, or find another source to borrow it.

As suggested earlier in this book, get the extra money out of your checking account and put it in a separate account that is harder to get to. If it takes time to go get it you won't spend it as easily.

Another technique is to do research when buying large items. Go to the public library and read *Consumer Reports* ratings of quality, service, amenities available, and pricing. Only buy the level of quality, the name brand, the service contracts, and the amount of bells and whistles you actually need. Don't overbuy or be oversold!

You need to control any penny "leaks." This is very important to your success. Many of our clients, having completed their first spending plan, will show that they should have a few hundred dollars left at the end of each month. That looks good on paper but when asked where it is they have no clue. Part of the real problem is they didn't use a set-aside account and keep getting hit with surprises for needing cash.

Avoid using credit unless it is an absolute emergency. Then find a way to pay all or most of it off at the end of the month to avoid interest.

It is important to start negotiating when you buy items or services. See if the vendor will take less.

Challenges to Overcome While Living the Survival Lifestyle

These challenges will have to be met to be successful in moving to the control lifestyle. When these roadblocks have been removed, you will find a smooth path offering a much easier transition to the next lifestyle.

While living at the survival level, one of the biggest challenges is to overcome a lack of self-confidence and achieve a positive attitude. These greatly affect you when it comes to being able to control, manage and attract money.

You will have to adopt a new belief system—one that helps you develop a high level of self-confidence and the belief that you are worthy of a better life, in addition to being able to do what it takes to make it happen. You must create the passion for change. Those who are successful in a reasonable time frame get help from a support group to become successful as well as develop a trust in their ability to make the necessary changes.

You must become frugal and be willing to live on a financial diet—one that is planned out. You can do it because you know this won't be forever. Just until you become healthy.

You need to accept the fact that you need change.

You must change your mind-set and the way you look at your money.

You have to make sure you don't revert to old habits of buying and living a drifting approach to finances. Be willing to change your financial focus to controlling and taking responsibility for your own destiny. Fully understand and take charge of your buying habits so you buy with your logical mind and not with your emotional mind as in the past. Learn the difference between wants and needs and only buy what you need. Move away from being an impulse and immediate gratification purchaser.

You must want the rewards you will get by living a higher lifestyle enough to be willing to keep records and track your growth. You will have to empower yourself to take control over your buying habits.

The challenge is for you to intervene, stop what you are doing, and change your spending habits. It will be an emotional challenge also, because not only do you have bad spending habits, but the way you operate financially defines you. For some people it can be a major psychological change to accept a "new you" when it comes to spending money and organizing your finances. You will have to replace your lack of willpower by developing the strength to not buy. The psychological reward needs to come from control and saving, not buying.

Another roadblock will be forcing yourself to pay attention to the details. The dollar "leaks" have to be recognized and plugged. You will also change the way you approach your finances. You must adapt methods for becoming organized. You have to be willing to do what it takes to pay all bills on time, putting a high priority on watching your finances, and getting and staying organized. You will have to start keeping track of your finances as never before. You no longer can operate by the cash you have in your pocket or by waiting for your next paycheck.

- You will have to commit to a bill-paying schedule.
- Be able to live by financially planning and scheduling your shopping trips.
- Your habit of enjoying short-term spontaneity in spending must be altered. For your allowance only.
- You must stop blaming others or bad luck for your financial condition.
- You will need to live under self-scrutiny.
- You will need to take full responsibility for future setbacks.
- You will need to take charge, make change happen, and not let it happen to you.

Chapter **EIGHT**

The Control Lifestyle

The characteristics of those living the control lifestyle

These are people who are living at their means but without any savings. They do their best to not waste money and pay all bills on time. The challenge is that funds are never available for any extras or emergencies. Many have a handle on their money but without a little more income they live in frustration.

They are in transition. The effort, time, and energy they devote to getting control of their finances will build the foundation for growing to whatever level they desire.

The people living in the control lifestyle want to be in charge of their finances. They have either had enough stress from living in the survival lifestyle or they have always been conservative and want control. They spend less time handling or running from collection agents or calls due to late pays.

They want to be more in control of what is happening to them financially. They need to know how much money is coming in and when and how much money is going out and when. Part of their motivation is their dislike for not knowing where their money is going. They are tired of not having enough money for emergencies or experiencing money shortages. They know if they only had some reserves their life would be more comfortable.

They stay focused on not wasting money. They refrain from using credit if possible. They are financially organized in order to pay their bills on time when possible. At this level there is no extra money; therefore, in case of a setback there are no reserves to solve the problem or need.

They begin to stop impulse buying. They stall the desire for immediate gratification. They also are aware of overconsumption. They start to live within their means. They focus on the money, but not in a negative way as many in the survival level do. They see the need for a financial diet. They don't know how to find extra money within their current income and expenses. They don't know where to cut or adjust their spending. Most of the folks we mentor are in this position. It seems more difficult than it really is.

Some people will stay locked into this control lifestyle forever. Others will want a better financial life and will begin to reach for more. They want to get out of the stress of living with heavy debt. They often feel frustrated from not being able to get ahead. If there is a couple with shared finances at this level they may face major problems if one is frugal and wants to change and the other is a high-consumption personality.

The Mind-Set of Those Living in the Control Lifestyle

These people need to understand and be willing to change their mind-set. This includes what they frequently think about, what worries them most, how they think about money, what motivates them, and how they handle stress.

People in this mind-set are constantly focusing on knowing where they stand financially. They will start to appreciate planning their spending and tracking their money. They believe to get ahead they must work more. They start to develop hope for a better financial future but don't really believe it will come. They may get bogged down because they don't have the experience or knowledge of how to change their thoughts and habits.

If you see yourself in the control lifestyle, open your mind to the rewards of living a higher lifestyle. Seek out some help; it will make your journey much shorter and less painful. Check our Web site at *www.creatingmoneyforlife.com.*

The Rewards Received by Living the Control Lifestyle

Control life-style people look for the tools and education to get turned around financially. They can start to believe they have an impact on their finances. The feeling of control is a powerful reward. They are willing to look for ways to lower their expenses by 10–20 percent. They are able to pay bills on time and they begin to have some savings—a blessing on its own. It creates a better feeling of financial self-worth and peace of mind. Many get frustrated with never seeming to be able to afford vacation and luxury items.

Those who know there is a better way seek education. If you are here and want a road map, go to our Web site, *www.creatingmoneyfor life.com.*

This road map lowers the frustration and embarrassment of not being able to pay bills on time and lessens time spent chasing dollars and worry.

Feeling Good about Being in Control

Lessons to be learned during the control lifestyle

You will need to learn how to set up and use a budget. You will need to learn your spending habits. To do this, please take this test to identify some of your important spending habits.

Please circle the ones that describe your behavior.

Test

1. I like to go shopping.
2. I read the ads in Sunday's newspaper.
3. I am an impulse buyer.
4. I am an immediate-gratification type person.
5. I buy as long as I feel I can afford the payment.
6. It is easy for me to use my credit cards.
7. I like to go to garage and other sales.
8. It feels good to buy.
9. I won't buy unless I have the money to pay off my credit cards at the end of the month.
10. I always take a break for a few days before making a buying decision.
11. I plan for large purchases and always save the money before I buy.

12. I have my money allocated in a envelope-type system.

The first eight items are bad habits that keep people from becoming financially healthy. To grow from the survival level, one must control behavior by changing buying habits. Numbers 9–12 are good habits and should be used constantly in order to stay on track financially.

You will have to learn how to focus differently on your money. You also will have to learn a new set of buying habits and strategies. You will want to become aware of the difference between wants and needs. It is important to learn to use the buyer-defense mechanisms provided later in this book.

You need to learn how to develop a budget/spending plan. In order to do this properly you need to understand the difference between debts and expenses, in addition to knowing the difference between fixed and variable expenses.

You need to learn the differences in regular, periodic, and unusual income. You need to learn to spend at a level that is consistent with your current capability and not on what you desire. An example is that you can buy a $10,000 watch or a $19.95 watch. You can take shut off showers to save money. You can buy a $65 blouse or a $10 blouse. You can spend a little on Christmas parties wth friends and relatives and give out small gifts. Or you can spend, like many of our students do, $1,000–$1,500 on gifts. Most of those gifts will be broken or forgotten within a few months.

Actions You Need to Take to be Successful in the Control Lifestyle

1. Invest the time it takes to set up your record-keeping system.

2. Set up a scheduled time each week and month to review your plans, results, and make needed adjustments for success.

3. Set up a budget/spending plan. Start living on your budget.

4. Begin living on a financial diet. Think about ways to focus on being frugal.

5. Set up your money-tracking systems and begin keeping adequate financial records.

6. Continue to use and develop even better buying-defense mechanisms.

7. Learn to understand and appreciate the "total income allocation" system.

8. Start to write down reasons for not buying before you buy anything.

9. Develop and practice decision-making skills for buying needs and avoiding buying wants.

10. Set up and use your 60-day daily money-tracking system. This will help you find money "leaks."

11. Fill out the work sheets for your set-aside account and adjust the monthly amount needed if necessary.

12. Fill out your set-aside account information. Plan for the next 12 months' wants and needs, total them, then divide it by 12 so you have the monthly amount needed to saving.

13. Review your income against total money going out. This will be your checks and balances on your cash flow.

14. Set up your allowance based on good financial

planning. Only approve yourself for an amount that leaves money for all other needs.

15. Adjust your budget and financial plans once you have established the budget, set-aside account, and allowance to create extra money each month.

16. Adjust your plan if your forecast indicates any negative cash flow.

17. Set up your bill-paying system to ensure you will not pay bills late.

18. Open your mind and be creative when considering means for increasing your income or lowering your expenses.

19. Review all expenses and list the ones you can cut out or reduce.

20. Set a goal for reducing all variable expenses by 10–20 percent over the next 60 days.

21. Review and find ways to create extra income if needed. Use the income advancement list in this book.

22. Find reduced or free recreation your family will enjoy, replacing more expensive hobbies.

Information and Ideas for Implementing the Actions Needed for the Control Lifestyle

Total Income Allocation System

This system is to plan out all of your income. It includes expenses and debt payments, set aside account needs, reserve and investment funding, and allowance. All income will be allocated to the proper categories. Your needs will all be met and you won't make late payments. It will keep you organized and on track for wealth. This system will keep you on track and will help you avoid leaks of your hard earned money. It will provide the willpower to not buy. It will ensure you are making the reserve and investments you need to reach your goals. As you grow financially you can add to your allowance. Eventually you will reach your goals and have all the fun money you want.

Plan and develop a budget

Your budget or spending plan has to start with your income. There are three kinds of income. Regular income—which you get from a job, Social Security, disability, child support or other—comes in at the same time and in the same amount each pay period. This is easy to plan around as long as it isn't interrupted.

Periodic income is income that comes in sporadically and the amount varies. This is from tips, commissions, bonuses, overtime, dividends, and so forth. This income, unless it is from your full-time job and only income, is more difficult to plan around than regular income. It can be done by using past income experiences, and being conservative with your estimates. In this day and age it is difficult, but this income—if over and above your regular income—should not be designated for covering normal debt and expenses every month. This should be the income to use for building reserves, accelerating debt elimination or investing.

The third type is unusual income. This is from tax returns, the sale of assets, inheritance or refunds. The problem with below-healthy-level living is that this income is used to catch up with overdue bills and often is part wasted as an ego relief from living day-to-day.

Make a list of all debts and expenses

The second step to budget planning is to list all the debts you pay each month and your expenses, using the best estimate of what you will be earning and spending for at least the next three months.

The third step is to fill out the set-aside account requirements to anticipate needs for the next 12 months. After the list is complete for the year it should be divided by 12 to get the monthly amount that needs to be set in reserve so the money will be available in the future.

The fourth step is to add the monthly set-aside amount to the total debt and expense for the total needed.

The fifth step is to take the regular income and subtract the total sum from the previous calculation, and you have just discovered you will have a negative or positive cash position at the end of the next month. Now that you know where you stand, you can make necessary adjustments.

If you are going to be negative it is better to know it now than at the end of the month when you run out of money before all bills have been paid. That short-notice surprise causes stress and often bad decisions. If you are negative or are anticipating less cash than wanted you can do one of two things: increase income or lower expenses.

If you need extra money—no matter if the purpose is for reserves, paying off debts early, investing or increasing your allowance, there are only two ways to get it. By increasing your income and/or lowering your expenses.

Here are some ideas to review. See if any will work for you.

Finding Extra Money

1. Increase your income.
   a. Receive raises.
   b. Get bonuses.
   c. Inherit money.
   d. Work overtime.
   e. Borrow from profit-sharing.
   f. Take a second job.
   g. Start a home business.
   h. Use the return on investments.
   i. Rent/lease assets you have.
   j. Sell assets you own.
2. Lower your expenses.
   a. Cut out any unneeded expenses.
   b. Redo expenses.
   c. Trade resources for expenses.
   d. Share expenses.
   e. Trade for lower price expenses/debts.
3. Redirect spending.
   a. Use coupons and discounts.
   b. Select where, when, how what, how often, and the quantities you buy.
   c. Buy quality equal to your needs.
   d. Take care of what you own
   e. Borrow or rent seldom-used items

Ways to Find Money and Help You Cash Flow

(Review the following list to see if you should use any of these. These are not suggested for all individuals.) Highlight the ones that might be useful for you, but don't implement them before carefully checking them out!

1. Change to credit cards with lower rates (read terms carefully).
2. Control the number and length of long-distance phone calls.
3. Get debtors to change your payment due date to avoid late fees.
4. If you have a computer use e-mail instead of long-distance phone.
5. Change to a lower rate long-distance phone carrier or use a phone card.
6. Buy your phones if you are still renting them.
7. Only use information service when necessary and dial the number yourself.
8. Unplug the extra refrigerator or freezer if you only have a few items in it.
9. Turn down the thermostat on your water heater.
10. If you plan on staying in your home for a while, change the showerhead and toilet to more efficient models.
11. If you have lights you leave on for more than four hours per day, change to compact fluorescent bulbs.
12. See if you still have a deposit with the utility company and if the time has past so you can get it back.
13. If you are planning on living in your current home for 10 years or more, change to more efficient heating and air-conditioning systems.
14. Shop around for life and disability insurance savings if you haven't done so in a few years.
15. Ask about insurance price breaks if you buy more than one type from the same vendor. Also, see if there are any discounts for belonging to a particu-

lar group. Check to see if rates can be lowered because of special circumstances.

16. Cut your home insurance by installing safety devices.
17. See about an umbrella liability insurance policy.
18. Raise the deductible on your insurance policies.
19. Buy national flood insurance if you live in a floodplain.
20. Buy only enough life insurance for funeral coverage for your small children.
21. Check out joining a health maintenance organization.
22. Check out employer plans that let you set aside pre-tax dollars for medical expenses not covered by insurance.
23. Stop smoking.
24. After you have quit smoking for a year see if your insurance rate can be lowered.
25. Don't buy higher octane fuel than your car needs.
26. Shop around frequently for car insurance.
27. Don't purchase a four-wheel drive vehicle unless you really need one.
28. When you buy your next car, only buy the extra options you need.
29. Buy a used car as opposed to new.
30. Watch for slow-moving models of cars and ask for a dealer discount.
31. Compare medicine prescription prices and ask the pharmacy to match the best prices.
32. Ask doctors to prescribe generic drugs when acceptable.
33. Ask retail stores for a discount on large items.

34. Wait for sales and off-season discounts when buying large items.
35. Plan ahead and allow ten days or longer to mail-order your commonly used prescriptions.
36. Buy generic over-the-counter drugs.
37. Compare eyeglass prices.
38. Get hospital itemized bills and check accuracy.
39. Buy in bulk.
40. Buy at discount outlets.
41. Always use a shopping list.
42. Don't grocery-shop when hungry.
43. Don't leave money needed for later bills in the checking account and falsely assume you can use it for something else.
44. Carry an updated price notebook for price comparisons on items you frequently buy.
45. Only buy what you really need.
46. Don't go shopping for recreation.
47. Stop reading the advertisements except for a particular item you need.
48. Use coupons.
49. Mail in rebates.
50. Don't use coupons if items are higher priced than alternatives you can buy.
51. Wait to buy landscape products until the season is partially gone or at the end.
52. Buy items that will last, such as coats, at the end of the season.
53. Use a debit card, not a credit card.
54. Use an ATM card instead of traveler's checks.
55. If you are in an area without ATMs, use a credit card for cash advances.

56. Alter your travel schedule to get the best pricing.
57. Use travel agents that book hotel rooms in bulk.
58. Trade your skills or knowledge for products or services you need.
59. Start a home-repair group. Once per month get together and work on each other's homes. Do the same with a babysitting trade group.
60. Pay your kids a bonus for finishing college early.
61. Start a home business that will require work your kids can do, and pay them wages as opposed to allowances, college funds, etc.
62. Don't use one-hour photo services or other convenience services.
63. Turn in unwanted photos at a processing store who will give you credit for them.
64. Check on reduced fees for home banking.
65. Get a brokerage fee reduction on stocks by buying online.
66. Donate for tax write-off or for cash unused items.
67. Take advantage of price wars.
68. Plan your income tax payments so you don't overpay throughout the year and make an interest-free loan to the IRS.
69. Take advantage of tax-deferred and employer-funded retirement investments.
70. Maximize 401(k) programs if employer matches funds.
71. Set up a file to track all expenses that can be used as tax write-offs.
72. Track all debt and bill payments to make sure you are not overcharged or pay twice.
73. Donate appreciated assets, not cash.

74. Negotiate with sellers of items when possible.
75. When you need an item, first consider borrowing or renting it, rather than buying it.
76. Buy infrequently used items with a group.
77. Use the library as opposed to buying books, tapes, and videos.
78. Use the yellow pages, phone, or internet to shop for comparisons.
79. Cancel subscriptions you don't use.
80. Go back to basic cable TV if you are not using the more expensive programming.
81. Don't buy lottery tickets.
82. Don't shop in convenience stores.

Next, project your budget out for three months. Go 12 months forward for even better planning.

Fill out your set aside form (see next page). This will give you the amount of money each month you need to cover your future wants and needs.

Set Up a Tracking System for Monitoring the Results

Once you have set up your annual budget, it is easy to create a chart or spreadsheet to watch the results of your income and expense predictions. Your chart should have a column for budgeted amounts and, next to it, a column for actual amounts that is to be filled in at the end of the month with what you actually paid for the expenses or debt, and a third column indicating the amount of change in dollars and cents. This change column will give you an accurate, timely, comparison figure from which to adjust your future monthly budget.

Set Aside Account Needs Form

Purpose: to have the needed funds available for future needs/wants

	Annual Amount Needed	Monthly Amount Needed	Due Dates
Home Purchase (closing costs/pre-paids)	_____	_____	_____
Children School	_____	_____	_____
Christmas/Gifts	_____	_____	_____
Auto Insurance (if not paid monthly)	_____	_____	_____
Life Insurance (if not paid monthly)	_____	_____	_____
Auto Maintenance (Repairs, oil changes, tires)	_____	_____	_____
Clothes	_____	_____	_____
Vacations	_____	_____	_____
Large Purchases	_____	_____	_____
Home Improvements	_____	_____	_____
Heating Bills	_____	_____	_____
Renter's Insurance	_____	_____	_____
Sewer/Water	_____	_____	_____
Others	_____	_____	_____
Total Amounts	_____	Divide by twelve to get monthly	

Savings Needs $ _____

After using these tools for a few months you will get a better sense of what is going to happen and when you will need to produce more income or cut expenses. The chart will also show where you might be able to accomplish the adjustment. It will also help you alleviate the financial surprises in your life and, better use extra income or savings. This will increase your ability—and shorten the time—to reach the next level of financial lifestyle.

Find money within your current income to get away from negative cash flow including your set-aside and allowance figures. Find a way to cut at least 10 percent out of your variable expenses. You will need to determine wants and needs, and establish new values as to what is truly important and right to buy in your current lifestyle.

Develop decision-making skills required to distinguish between wants and needs and to comparison shop for goods and services.

> *Make sure you understand the difference between your wants and needs.*
>
> ***Needs*** *are essentials, the basics of life: Think food, clothing, and a place to live.*
>
> ***Wants*** *simply increase the quality of living. These are goods and services that add comfort; ego feeds that add fun and pleasure but are not needed to survive.*

Your values will play an important part in how you see the difference between needs and wants. Your values are defined as what is right and what is important to you.

Daily Tracking for 60 Days!

If you are living paycheck to paycheck or you run out of money before all bills are paid then you need to track all expenditures (purchases) for the next two months.

Keep daily and weekly totals. You will begin to see patterns and cash "leaks." Pennies daily turn into dollars weekly, grow into hundreds of dollars monthly, and become thousands of dollars lost in a year.

Remember that your financial well-being, not accumulating stuff, should be a top priority when it comes to buying. Your decisions—what to buy, when to buy, how much to buy—should be based on the following:

1. Is it for me or my family's survival?
2. Is getting the item or service needed because it is an emergency?
3. Did I budget or have the item or service in my set-aside account?
4. Is the item or service within my budget?
5. Do I have to charge it to buy it?
6. Would it be better for my financial well-being to establish a new goal for obtaining the item or service?
7. What quality level, name recognition, and amenities do I really need?
8. What are the consequences to my budget, goals achievement, and financial future if I buy now?
9. Can I live with the consequences? What will it cost

Weekly Log (use when you spend ANY money)

Date	Time	Item	Vendor	Amount

me in stress, budget adjustment, late fees, interest payment, and thwarting my goal achievement?

10. Are there any alternatives such as deferring the purchase, borrowing or renting the item, trading for the service, etc.?

Stop letting lenders own you. Learn to save and pay cash.

When the decision is made to go ahead with the purchase, consider comparison shopping.

Comparison Shop

1. Look at only the level of quality and bells and whistles you need.

2. Shop around for the best terms and price. (Use the phone first before running around to stores.)

3. Do research on brand names, models, and service records when possible.

4. Use your local public library for *Consumer Reports* research.

5. Look for discounts and sales.

6. Use coupons when practical.

7. Talk to others about service level of retailers or service vendors.

8. Buy when the item is offered with a rebate if it is the best price you can find. Make sure you commit to mail in the rebate.

You need to start with a daily tracking system that will have a positive effect on your impulse buying and will give you the tracking needed to see where you are suffering from cash "leaks."

You need a good understanding of your buying habits and who is currently controlling your financial decisions.

You will need to understand and implement a set-aside account system for predicting future want and need expenditures. A part of this is to use the tool of establishing an allowance formula.

You will need to adjust your spending to re-allocate at least $100 to properly utilize of your money.

You will need to establish a bill-paying system to make sure you no longer are paying bills or debts late.

Learn to use more logical than emotional decision making when buying. Learn defensive thoughts and techniques to stop impulse and immediate-gratification buying patterns.

Keeping Adequate Financial Records

Why should you keep adequate financial records?

1. To stay financially organized
2. To stay focused on your spending plan (budget) versus your actual spending
3. To keep track of unpaid bills so you avoid late payments and penalties
4. To keep focused on your other financial goals in order to measure results
5. To create easy access to your income tax deductions and credits when needed
6. To have someone be able to take over your finances in case of emergency
7. To use for making financial plan adjustments in a timely manner

8. To have records from which to compare current situations to old habits and situations

9. To be able to readily check bills and bank statements for accuracy

10. To have quick access to challenge bill-paying discrepancies.

What Financial Records Should you Keep?

1. Unpaid bills

2. Paid bill receipts and cancelled checks

3. Tax-deductible receipts

4. Bank statements

5. Receipts for large purchases

6. Active service agreements and warranties

7. Forms provided throughout this course for planning and tracking purposes

8. Employer W2s

9. Pay stubs

10. Receipts for contributions

11. Past tax returns

12. Investment documents such as 401(k), IRA, etc.

How Should You Organize Your Receipts?

1. Keep all critically important records and financial documents in a safety deposit box—either a bank-rented box or a home fireproof safe.

2. For current records and ones frequently used as

comparisons of plans and goals to the actual, keep them at home in an easy-to-locate file.

3. You can stay organized by computer software or a manual file system. A manual system can be kept in a file cabinet or the right size cardboard box.

4. You should keep two files in addition to the bank safety deposit box.

5. Keep one for active files containing information for easy access. This file should be kept at least for three years. The second file is a dead storage file to keeping long-term information. The active file section should include the following records for up to three years and then be moved to the dead file.

   a. unpaid bills

   b. paid bill receipts

   c. current cancelled checks

   d. current bank statements

   e. income tax working papers

   f. tracking records for spending plans and financial goals

   g. payment tracking schedule from workbook

Tips

1. Review dead file records at least annually and delete any unnecessary documents.

2. Keep all records that are confidential and potentially an identity theft risk in a secured place.

3. Review bank statements and bills for accuracy when you receive them.

Payment Tracking Schedule

For the Month of: _____

Week 1

Source	Due Date	Budget Amount	Actual Amount
		$	$
		$	$
		$	$
		$	$
		$	$
		$	$
		$	$
		$	$
		$	$
Totals $		$	$

Week 2

Source	Due Date	Budget Amount	Actual Amount
		$	$
		$	$
		$	$
		$	$
		$	$
		$	$
		$	$
		$	$
		$	$
Totals $		$	$

Week 3

Source	Due Date	Budget Amount	Actual Amount
		$	$
		$	$
		$	$
		$	$
		$	$
		$	$
		$	$
		$	$
		$	$
Totals $		$	$

Week 4

Source	Due Date	Budget Amount	Actual Amount
		$	$
		$	$
		$	$
		$	$
		$	$
		$	$
		$	$
		$	$
		$	$
Totals $		$	$

Take-Home Income

	Budget	Actual
Week 1	$	$
Week 2	$	$
Week 3	$	$
Week 4	$	$
Totals	$	$

Set-Aside Account

	Budget	Actual
Week 1	$	$
Week 2	$	$
Week 3	$	$
Week 4	$	$
Totals $		$

Cash Flow

	Budget	Actual	Difference
Week 1	$	$	
Week 2	$	$	
Week 3	$	$	
Week 4	$	$	
Totals $		$	

Deposits

YTD Set-Aside Account _____

YTD Savings Account _____

Monthly Extras:

Source	Amount	Due Date	Set-Aside / Savings

4. Balance your checkbook every time you make a debit or credit entry.

5. Balance your checkbook monthly when you get the bank statement.

6. Use the workbook page for paying bills on time.

7. Track your set-aside account monthly for changes in your anticipated expenditures to make timely adjustments to your spending plan.

8. Implement and use a payment tracking schedule system.

Budgeting Starts with Income!

How much comes in, where does it come from (source), and when does it come in?

—Regular
—Variable (periodic—commission, tips, bonuses, overtime, dividends)
—Unusual or one-time (gifts, sale of assets, inheritance)

- Begin to live on regular income only and use the other incomes to get ahead.
- List all your current debt payments, fixed and variable expenses for a month. Make a chart.
- Set up your financial tracking tools.
- Add your total outgo for a month.
- Make your set-aside account and add the needed monthly savings to the total outgo.

Now you know what your total current monthly income needs have to be. Compare the total outgoing money to your regular income—do you have positive or negative cash flow? How will you adjust?

Develop your spending and set-aside account plans and calculate whether you will have positive or negative cash at the end of each month. Do this for at least the next three months. Review your plans to make necessary adjustments. If you have negative cash flow, there is only two things you can do. Cut expenses or add income.

Go through your list of variable expenses and find 10 percent that you can cut from those expenses.

Make a chart of your debts. List the amounts owed, the minimum monthly payments, the interest accounts and the due dates.

Learn the formula for paying off debts in seven to nine years and use it to set up your debt-elimination plan. Use the stacking method.

Learn to read, interpret, and clean up your credit report. Learn to use credit wisely and keep your credit score as high as possible.

The Wise Use of Credit

You need to know the types, sources and costs of credit and loans. There are basically two types of consumer loans:

1. *Revolving*—the credit for which you are qualified for a maximum amount of money. You can borrow against the line of credit any time you want as long as you have an available amount. Your credit limit will be the most you can borrow on that line of credit.

Revolving credit means you can borrow against the credit line, pay it down, and borrow again.

2. *Installment loans*—these are monies you borrow that are one-time loans on the amount you borrowed. You will pay principal and interest on the loan until it is paid in full. One example is a car loan. Once you borrow the money it is not a line of credit to borrow against as you pay some of the principal down.

There are also secured and unsecured loans. Secured means you pledged some security or assets to protect the lender. In the event of default the lender has the legal right to take the security as part or all of the repayment. Unsecured means you borrowed the money on your signature alone without backing it up with any specifically assigned assets.

The sources of loans are:

1. Credit unions
2. Mortgage companies
3. Banks
4. Savings and loan associations
5. Consumer finance companies
6. Credit card companies
7. Retail stores
8. Pawnbrokers
9. Friends and relatives
10. Life insurance companies
11. Check-cashing stores
12. Payday loans
13. Rent-to-own stores (not technically a loan)
14. Sale finance companies

Cost of Credit

Depending on the type and source of loan, the borrower will pay up-front fees, finance charges, annual fees, interest, and some times prepayment penalties.

The federal Truth in Lending Act requires lenders to state their interest charges as an annual percentage rate (APR) so that consumers can compare true costs of borrowing.

What Should You be Aware of as Debt Warning Signs?

1. Borrowing to pay for personal expenses
2. Borrowing small amounts that you can't pay off at the end of the month
3. When your credit balances are increasing
4. Attempting to get new credit from many sources due to getting turned down
5. Interest payments are over your budgeted amount and/or your goal
6. When you are paying late fees due to lack of money to pay bills
7. When your total debt payments are too high for you to handle

What are Some Appropriate Uses of Credit?

1. Credit can be used for buying large items such as a home or car.
2. Credit can be used in times of emergency.

3. Credit is sometimes safer than carrying or using cash.

4. Credit cards are sometimes needed for situations such as hotel or car rentals.

5. Credit, when used properly, will help build or provide a high credit score.

6. Credit can be used to pay bills, but should be paid off each month.

7. Credit can be used to keep track of your purchases.

8. Credit can be used to take advantage of reward programs, i.e., free flight tickets.

9. Credit purchases are sometimes protected by the lender in the event of products not represented properly, broken or not received as agreed upon.

What Alternatives are There to Using Credit?

1. Wait until you have the cash to pay for the item.

2. Borrow from your set-aside account if it is an emergency, but only after you have created a realistic plan to repay it in time to cover your future money needs.

3. Borrow the item from a friend or relative.

4. Find some other means to solve the problem.

5. Trade services or assets you own for the item.

6. Sell some assets or your knowledge, skills, and time to get the money needed to purchase the item.

7. Increase your income or lower expenses to provide the money for the purchase.

Set up your tracking systems that will tell you at the beginning of each month whether you will have negative or positive cash. Fill out the forms at the end each month comparing budget to actual so you can use the difference to adjust your budget for the upcoming months. Develop the sensibility and interest level you need to keep a close watch over your finances.

The Challenges to Overcome While Living in the Control Lifestyle

The following challenges will have to be met to be successful during the control lifestyle and to provide a smooth transition into the healthy lifestyle.

- You will need to become more logical and less emotional about your finances. You will need to control your buying decisions. Take the position to act and not react to buying situations.
- You will need to understand, become comfortable with, and use buying-defense mechanisms.
- You will have to think more logically when it comes to analyzing whether a purchase decision is based on want or need, in addition to deciding if it fits your spending plan.
- You will need to create a passion for controlling your finances. The activities that seemed a pain in the past will have to be part of an important structural change if you are to succeed.
- You must make a commitment to tracking your financial activities and results. You will have to be sen-

sitive to how much money is coming in and when, and how much is going out and when.

- You will have to open your mind to create the desire for planning your financial future. Stop seeing your world as of today only.
- You will need to develop the willpower to stay on your spending plan.
- You must create the desire for saving money.
- You will need to change your mind-set to be able to function within your budget. You must be willing to handle the stress of sticking to your spending plan, including funding your set-aside account and allowance.
- You must take on the challenge to alter your lifestyle by enjoying less-costly hobbies and recreation. You must recognize and be willing to keep yourself out of places that offer opportunities to buy.
- You will need to change to a passion for staying on track rather than shopping and spending.
- You must alter your attitude about the amount of paperwork or computer work it takes to keep in control so you won't burn out.
- You must open your mind to wanting a higher level lifestyle.
- You will need to build your self-confidence and feelings of self-worth in order to grow.
- You will need to learn to enjoy a total income allocation forecast system.
- You will begin to trust, enjoy, and you must stay within your "Total Income Allocations" system. Realize the only free spending money comes from your allowance, not from other categories.

Chapter NINE

The Healthy Lifestyle

The characteristics of those living the healthy lifestyle

The typical characteristics of those living the healthy lifestyle are as follows:

- They are living within their means and have extra money in savings and reserves.
- They have between 1 percent and 25 percent of their income over and above what they need to survive.
- They have credit card balances, but are able to pay on time and keep their balances below 50 percent of the credit limit. This factor helps them keep a reasonably good credit rating, which helps when they want to borrow money.
- Their compulsion to spend during the survival level turns into a compulsion to be careful with their money.

- They do research before making large purchases to get the best value for their money and only the level of amenities they need. They know the difference between needs and wants. They aren't oversold by salespeople.
- They look to the future. Most are worried about their ability to live comfortably when they retire. They will start to calculate assets needed for future retirement. They develop discipline in spending. If two people share their finances they usually agree on whether or not to make large purchases.

  Some who have failed to look beyond the healthy lifestyle often will begin to panic and have anxiety when they start to get close to retirement.
- They start to see financial growth and enjoy accelerating debt pay-off.
- They have car and house payments that are in balance with their income level. Their debt-to-income level is in balance. However, they haven't yet become totally aware of how much their debt is hurting their financial future, so they keep using credit.

  Their net worth is growing—not because of much investing but due to paying down debt balances.
- They are paying down debts by using extra cash flow and not merely paying the minimum required payment each month.
- They put a little extra in their IRA or 401(k) each year.
- They often keep extra money each month in a CD (certificate of deposit) or in their money-management account.

- They increase the money they have for their allowance to have more fun money. They take vacations and get involved in somewhat costly recreational events and hobbies. They have created more money for saving and buying large items. They can find the funds to adjust to any expense changes and financial surprises. They are more frugal than those living in a control lifestyle.
- They have accumulated assets (the things they own and control), and they have debts or liabilities (what they owe).

  At the healthy level they have money to belong to a gym or exercise facility. They have learned to lower their expenses so they have extra money to work on getting out of debt, though most don't know how to accomplish it effectively. They are almost free of impulse and immediate-gratification spending except for an occasional small item. They begin to see the need for sacrifice-type living. They know that sacrifice gives them budget comfort, keeps them out of trouble, and can lead to a higher financial lifestyle.
- They focus on saving, paying down debt, and having reserves rather than spending every penny they get. They are more at peace with their money because they aren't worried about the next bill coming in or the landlord they are paying late. They can pay their debts. Many start to wish they hadn't taken on the level of debt they have. It becomes a burden and those who feel it often are the ones who want to take action to reduce or eliminate their debts. This begins a mind-set shift to-

ward the prosperity level. Hurray for those who
take action!

- They make better buying decisions than those on
the lower levels of personal financial management.
They buy used cars and or keep cars longer. They
learn to live slightly below their means. They stop
spending money thoughtlessly. They will think more
about buying appreciating assets—those assets that
will grow in value. They will spend less on depreciating assets.
- They operate within their budget. They buy out of
season, on sale, with coupons and on double-
coupon days. They don't care about what the Joneses
are buying or own. They anticipate money needs
rather than reacting to them.
- They begin to work from plans. They have established and are operating within their spending plan.
They create a set-aside plan for future needs and
wants. They develop a debt elimination program.
They also begin to implement tracking systems so
they can follow their progress in reaching their
goals. They establish benchmark goals along the way.
They work their plans. They control and stay on
track every day, and when they slip back into old
habits they quickly adjust and get back on their new
path to wealth. They will keep good financial
records, frequently and consistently tracking their
results.
- They understand the importance of having high
credit scores and will work toward improving their
rating.

The Mind-set of Those Living the Healthy Lifestyle

You will need to understand and be willing to change your mind-set. This includes what you frequently think about, what worries you most, how you think, what motivates you, and how you handle stress.

In the healthy lifestyle people have a tendency to worry about losing their job because it represents most of their needed income—losing it would mean financial disaster.

They stay focused on saving and paying off debt. They want growth but often operate from fear of loss. They feel they have worked hard for what they have and don't have a good feeling about how to reproduce their assets in the event they lose them. They don't understand the multiple streams of income concept. They don't have the knowledge or skills to quickly build passive income. They don't spend enough time learning about or looking for investments. They don't trust their investment instincts. They often listen to the naysayers and, therefore, don't act on opportunities. The influencing maysayers are always living their level of lifestyle or below. Prosperous and wealthy people have gotten that way by taking action and risk. They miss many opportunities. They overanalyze investments, looking for reasons not to get involved.

Many people get stuck at the healthy level because it can be comfortable enough. The problem is that they have enough income to pay debts and expenses but will they have enough in the future? Most of the healthy level will survive on social security only when their earned income stops. Their debts are eating away at their future. With some minor intervention they could enjoy a wealthy retirement.

The Rewards of the Healthy Lifestyle

Those living the healthy lifestyle will plan for vacations through their set-aside account. They will have money available to take a luxury vacation once in a while without charging it.

They are rewarded by watching their debt being reduced and headed for total elimination. At this stage they start to feel control over the lenders. In the past, they felt the debt controlled their money.

They will enjoy having more fun money and buying a few more items with cash. They are able to buy a few things for themselves that they will really enjoy such as shoes, a fishing rod, and so forth—things they didn't feel they could afford in the past.

Display paid-off debts on your refrigerator or in a prominent place. Begin to see real progress in paying off your debts. Observe your savings/investing plan starting to take shape, having more cash available than ever before. Feel good about being able to create your financial future. Understand what your credit scores are and how to improve and keep them in a good range. You will enjoy the benefit of having good credit. It is an ego feed to know you have high credit scores. You will be treated by lenders with greater respect.

You will have peace of mind from having cash reserves. You will feel good about watching your net worth grow. This makes you want to invest more. It feels good to have put off immediate gratification and impulse buying for future gains. For more help, see us at *www.creatingmoneyforlife.com*.

You will better understand what is meant by paying yourself first. You will do so. You will be able to take better advantage of your employer-matched 401(k) funds. You will find it much easier to put 5–10 percent of income into savings and investing. You will begin to see investments grow and take advantage of moneymaking opportunities. You will also begin to understand and be aware of ways to save money and start to cut taxes.

You will start to take real control of your money and financial planning thanks to having the extra money needed to make some serious adjustments. You will begin to turn the seven money controls hierarchy upside down. You will have found money in your current income to accelerate the debt pay-off plan.

You will have money to take nice vacations. You will have peace of mind thanks to having learned to ignore what the Joneses are buying or own. Your will also have peace of mind thanks to having cash reserves, though small at this level. You are now taking control and can easily make adjustments to your budgets when unexpected events happen that affect your cash flow. You are temporarily happy with small savings and investing dollars. You will become your own coach and cheerleader for paying off debt and getting ahead. You will feel better and improve your attitude and self-confidence when dealing with money.

Lessons to Learn While Living the Healthy Lifestyle

You must learn the importance of paying yourself first. You must learn how to write, implement, and work toward reaching your own smart goals. You will need to break down goals into benchmarks for measuring results and meeting deadlines.

You will need to learn the formula for calculating your net

worth. Once you know your net worth, you can compare it to what you should have in appreciating assets at this point in your life. It will also be a benchmark for planning and tracking your appreciating asset building plan, thus giving you a way to see if you are on track with the income-producing assets you will need.

You will want to learn to calculate your financial retirement needs. You will need to learn how to use the formula for your forecast money needs and calculate an amount you need to invest each month.

You will need to read, analyze, and possibly dispute your credit report. You will have to learn how to dispute any inaccurate information on your credit report.

You will learn how to run your finances like a profitable business. You will be able to make sound financial decisions based on your balance sheet/net worth, profit and loss statement and cash-flow forecast. The first document and tool is a balance sheet. It provides a picture of the net worth. This is critical for asset growth tracking and planning. This will create one's future income.

The second document is a profit and loss statement. This is a planning and tracking tool that predicts and audits the amount of money coming in and going out. It will show how much is needed. It also will provide the information to use for good buying decisions.

The third document is the cash-flow statement. This shows that at the end of the month you will either have positive cash left over or you will be negative and need more income or fewer expenses in order to break even.

Using the profit and loss and cash-flow documents will show how accurate your estimates were and if you are functioning the way you need to be in order to be healthy and beyond. These documents will show the extra cash that will be coming in for reserves, and raises in your allowance, savings, or investing.

Without using these three financial tools you are drifting and not operating from a good plan. This information must be available in a timely, accurate, comparative format to be useful.

You will have to adjust to being out of your comfort zone at first until you learn how to use financial tools that are new to you.

You will learn how to make sound financial decisions based on accurate and timely information in a time frame that fits your goals. Learn to not be complacent with having small amounts of reserves and paying debts on time or a little extra. You need the mind-set to want true progress.

You will need to track your liabilities to calculate whether or not they are too heavy for your income to support. They also need to be part of the plan to eliminate what isn't creating income potential.

Make sure you understand and invest in appreciating assets and not in depreciating assets. Your bank statement looks at total assets. My way of thinking is that the clothes, TVs, computers, cell phones, cars, and other non-appreciating assets have no future value and should be left out of your calculations.

Actions You Must Take to be Successful in the Healthy Lifestyle

In the healthy lifestyle you must function financially and plan and track financial information—just like a successful and profitable business.

1. Pay yourself first. Start arranging your budget today so that you have your savings and debt-reduction money planned for in your set-aside account. Take it off the top monthly and use it for paying off debts.

2. Write at least six financial goals and give them the smart test.

3. Write a plan for reaching your financial "SMART" goals for annual income, amount to pay down on debt, amount to put in reserve and investments, amount to reduce home expenses. Set up benchmarks with deadlines for progress tracking.

4. Calculate your current net worth.

5. Break out your appreciating assets from the depreciating assets.

6. Review your budget and set-aside accounts for accuracy and timeliness, and compare them with other tracking records.

7. Calculate your future income needs based on living comfortably in your retirement years.

8. Find extra money in your budget or added income to accelerate the payoff based on your goals.

9. Set up your results tracking system so you can watch your progress.

10. Start using the three business forms (profit and loss, cash flow, and balance sheet) for making buying and adjustment decisions.

11. Start on a debt-elimination program. Use the debt-elimination form to list your debts. Reconstruct the debt payments in order to accelerate the payoff.

12. Learn to read, interpret, and clean up your credit report.

13. Use creative thinking to find other sources of income and ways to reduce or eliminate more expenses.

14. Get a copy of your credit report, read it, and start disputing the inaccurate information.

15. Dispute all inaccurate information.

16. Shift savings to a 401(k) or IRA.

17. Read financial magazines for investing ideas.

18. Re-work your set-aside account.

19. Design your debt elimination plan and start paying off debts.

20. Start a credit dispute system.

21. Develop your credit repair dispute log to control the progress.

22. Comparison shop for annual renewal services such as insurance. Learn to place the money you save from comparison shopping into your debt-reduction plan.

23. Establish or add to your IRAs and your 401(k) or 403(b) and take advantage of any employer contribution matching-funds programs.

25. Create your plan to get out of debt.

26. Get insurance needs and premiums in line with what you need. First, review insurance coverage to make sure it is what you need. Get quotes to see if you can get the same coverage for lower premiums.

27. Read books, magazines, and news articles on investing and money management at the beginning level.

28. Review and adjust your "Total Income Allocation" system as you reach higher discretionary dollar levels.

29. Review the level of your allowance and increase it if it makes sense.

30. Get educated on how to use a financial calculator.

Information and Ideas for Implementing the Actions Needed to be Successful in the Healthy Lifestyle

Goal-setting and tracking

Goal-setting process

1. Identify your goal—make a list of goals you have identified and prioritize them.

   a. What is most important to you?

   b. What sequence in time are your goals likely to occur?

   c. Are there any competing goals? (Check against your budget.)

2. Write your goals down, making sure they are "SMART" goals and not dreams.

   SMART goals are the only ones that will work. All others are New Year's resolutions or hopes and dreams. They are not real achievable or measurable goals.

   S = Specific, **M** = Measurable, **A** = Attainable, **R** = Realistic, **T** = Timed.

Specific usually means the goal can be easily defined. Measurable means it usually has a result that can be tested by a number answer. Attainable means it has a high chance of being achieved. Realistic means it fits in with other goals and activities, and it won't negatively affect other areas of one's life. Timed means the goal has to have a deadline to be able to see if it was met.

A SMART goal is one that meets the test of all five criteria. If only one is left out, your chances of success are minimized. If you want to lose 10 pounds by January 5 of a certain year, your goal meets all five tests. Just merely saying that you want to lose some weight soon is not a SMART goal. See the difference?

3. List the specific dates for achieving each goal.

4. Break your goals into short-, medium-, and long-term.

5. Break goals into smaller achievement benchmarks by desired results and completion dates.

6. Establish and make a chart showing each of your financial goals. These should indicate start date, your final goal, total amount needed, date completed, amount needed weekly, bi-weekly, or monthly to meet your goals. List the actions to be taken to accomplish your goals.

7. Keep written goals in view so you can review them frequently.

8. Stay focused and determined.

9. Measure your progress. Set up your tracking system.

10. Reward yourself for success.

Here are the six financial goals everyone should learn to write, believe in, and go after. They need to be broken into small segments and written with deadline benchmarks.

1. Budget/spending goals

2. Savings/investing goals

3. Debt reduction/elimination goals

4. Credit rating goals

5. Credit clean-up goals

6. Results tracking goals

Review frequently results and reward yourself for reaching your benchmarks. To keep on track, make sure you review your results against the benchmarks and reward yourself for successes along the way.

Learn how to calculate your net worth. In doing so, you will fully understand the difference between appreciating assets and depreciating assets. Be able to relate your current net worth to where you should be in order to retire comfortably.

Goal tracking

1. Annual income (take home) $_____

2. Amount of savings in reserve $_____

3. Net worth $_____

4. Amount of debt (total) $_____

5. Amount of debt to reduce this year $_____

6. Total monthly home expenses $_____

7 Number of months of savings you
   want in reserve   _____

8. Total appreciating assets (from net worth form)
   $_____

9. Debt to equity ratio $_____

Net Worth Component Definitions:

Your assets are what you own.
Your liabilities are what you owe.
The difference is your net worth.

Formula for Calculating Your Net Worth

Net Worth Calculation Form

Assets		Liabilities	
Cash on hand	_____		
Value of house	_____	Balance owed on house	_____
		Balance owed on equity line	_____
Value of vehicles	_____	Balance owed on vehicles	_____
Value of personal items	_____	Balance owed on credit cards	_____
Value of stocks & bonds	_____	Balance owed on other loans	_____
TOTAL	_____	TOTAL	_____

Subtract liabilities from assets = $ _____ = Net Worth

Assuming you can get a reasonably safe 6 percent return from mutual funds or municipal bonds, you can expect $500 per month income for every $100,000 you have invested.

The financial planners tell us that most people will need 80 percent of their income for retirement after they factor in inflation. Take that figure and reduce it by pension income, Social Security income, inheritance-produced income, and any disability income. This will be the amount your assets need to produce.

In addition to maintaining your lifestyle you must plan for long term care. The 80% rule doesn't cover nursing care if Medicare or Medicaid can't be utilized.

Debt Reduction and Elimination

Most of our clients have too much debt. They have a high debt-to-income ratio. They are debt-payment strapped. They could retire early and have a much healthier financial life if they were out of debt. They also could reach the prosperity or wealth level with the money they are paying out each month for debt.

After teaching hundreds of clients how to accelerate the debt payoff program, I know that most people don't realize it can be done, how to calculate, or how to organize their debt payments to speed up paying off debts. Almost 100 percent of our clients could eliminate their total debt, including their house mortgage in seven to nine years. However, without a plan they continue to pay the normal way and will be paying on debt—in many cases—forever. Some minimum required payments are interest-only.

Another common mistake we see is clients paying a little extra off on the wrong loan. While this is better than not paying extra, they are not paying on the right debt to speed up the process in the fastest and most psychologically advantageous way.

A good motivator is for you to add up the total that you pay out each month on debt, including principal and interest. Next, ask yourself what you could use that money for if it weren't paying debt. If you calculate what it would do for you in accumulating wealth, it could help you retire early or have a much higher income or be used for investing and bringing you into the wealth/financial-freedom lifestyle.

Most people we work with are making at least $1,500 in debt payments. What would happen if they were debt free and wanted to retire in ten years. The $1,500 invested monthly at 8% return in stocks and bonds would become $276,249 value. If they invested the $1,500 per month in real estate at 25% return. They would have a future value of $799,207. Of they could continue to pay the debt for the next ten years and have nothing. Sorry to be so harsh. I don't want this to be your wake up call.

Debt control

Sources of Debt (creditors)	Credit Limit	Current Balance Owed	Debt-to-limit Ratio	Interest Rate	Minimum Payment
_____	_____	_____	_____	_____	_____
_____	_____	_____	_____	_____	_____
_____	_____	_____	_____	_____	_____
_____	_____	_____	_____	_____	_____
_____	_____	_____	_____	_____	_____
_____	_____	_____	_____	_____	_____
_____	_____	_____	_____	_____	_____
_____	_____	_____	_____	_____	_____
_____	_____	_____	_____	_____	_____
_____	_____	_____	_____	_____	_____
_____	_____	_____	_____	_____	_____

Total Debts $_____   Total Minimal Payments $_____

What could you do with the total payment amount each month? Yes, invest it!

How to Get Out of Debt

The Stack-Your-Payment Method

Debt	Amount Owed	Payment	Interest %	Years to Pay Off
Credit card 1	5,000	50	9.9	17.75
Credit card 2	3,500	58	20.0	NEVER
Car	6,000	250	4.0	2.17
Credit Union	2,000	75	8.0	2.5
House	100,000	650	6.5	27.67
Total Payments		1,083		

These clients revised their payment schedule and added $200 a month as a debt elimination accelerator. The new amount of money paid each month will now be $1,283. Instead of getting out of debt in 27.67 years they now will be debt free in 8.08 years.

Debt	Amount Owed	Payment	Interest %	Old Years to Pay Off	New Years to Pay Off
Credit union	2,000	275	8	2.5	8 months
Credit card 2	3,500	333	20	NEVER	1 year
Credit card 1	5,000	383	9.9	17.75	14 months
Car	6,000	250	4	2.17	paid off
House	100,000	1,283	6.5	27.67	8.08 years

The following formula is a rough example of what your monthly payments need to be to pay off your debts by a certain time. Look down the left column and see your total debt. Next, look at the monthly payment amount and look up to the number of years at the top of the payment column. You will see how long it will take you to get out of debt. You can use this for a planning tool to add an accelerator to your debt pay-off plan, and set a goal to be debt-free in a certain number of years. This is, of course, rough, because it is based on a blender interest rate for all debts. To have it exact, use a financial calculator or contact us for a true forecast at *www.creatingmoneyforlife.com*.

Debt Elimination Formula

Total Debts	1yr.	2yrs.	3yrs.	4yrs.	5yrs.	6yrs.	7yrs.	8yrs.
$2,000	176	92	65	51	43	37	33	30
$2,500	220	115	81	63	53	46	42	38
$3,000	264	138	97	76	64	56	50	46
$5,000	438	231	161	51	92	78	68	61
$8,000	703	369	258	203	170	148	133	121
$10,000	879	461	323	254	212	185	166	152
$15,000	1,319	692	484	380	319	278	249	228
$20,000	1,758	923	645	507	425	371	332	303
$30,000	2,637	1,384	968	761	637	556	498	455
$50,000	4,396	2,307	1,613	1,268	1,062	926	830	759
$100,000	8,792	4,614	3,227	2,536	2,125	1,853	1,600	1,517
$125,000	10,989	5,768	4,033	3,170	2,656	2,316	2,975	1,897
$150,000	13,187	6,922	4,840	3,804	3,187	2,779	2,490	2,276
$200,000	17,583	9,229	6,453	5,073	4,249	3,705	3,320	3,035
$250,000	21,979	11,536	8,067	6,341	5,312	4,631	4,150	3,794
$300,000	26,375	13,843	9,680	7,609	6,374	5,558	4,980	4,552
$350,000	30,771	16,151	11,294	8,877	7,484	6,484	5,810	5,311

Current monthly debt payments: $_____

When will you be out of debt with your current
monthly payments, including accelerator?   _____

How many years until you want to be out of debt?   _____

Check amount you need to pay to reach your goals: $ _____

Definitions of the Three Financial Tools

1. Balance Sheet—assets minus liabilities = net worth
2. Profit and Loss = your income vs. your monies going out
3. Cash Flow = money left after debts, expenses, reserves, and set-aside account needs are satisfied

You need a plan for each of the three financial systems in order to succeed financially. You have a choice of how you want your finances to be—operating at a loss, survival level, or wealth— it's up to you!

Credit Report Scores and Cleanup

How does your poor credit rating (score) affect you?

1. Limits your ability to borrow.
2. Costs you much more in higher interest rates.
3. It can cause you to qualify for less home. Or cause you to come up with a much higher down payment.
4. It can limit your financial flexibility (type of mortgage, mortgage insurance).
5. It can drastically reduce your buying/investing power.
6. It can get you turned down for leasing a house or an apartment.
7. It can keep you from getting a job.
8. It can give you higher auto insurance premiums.

9. It can cause more stress by creating more problems in getting a loan.

10. It can keep you from investing with no money down.

11. It can slow you down from becoming financially free.

Do you know what your score is today? _____

Credit report/repair

Tips:
- Show stability in payments, addresses, and employment.
- Keep open three to six lines of credit: two credit cards, one store account, one gas card, and maybe one installment loan.
- Keep balances under 50 percent of the credit limit; 35 percent is even better and will help your score.

Fair Isaac (FICO) scoring

Payment History = 35 percent (recent late pays are bad—late 60/90 days is worse)

Amounts Owed = 30 percent (limit to balance ratio; 35 percent or better is best)

Length of Credit = 15 percent

New Credit = 10 percent (negative impact)

Type of Credit = 10 percent (high-risk types are negative)

Free annual credit reports

Visit *www.annualcreditreport.com* or call 877-322-8228.

Disputing credit report entries

Types of errors frequently found on credit reports which should be disputed:

1. Not my account
2. Never paid late
3. Released in bankruptcy
4. Paid in full
5. Paid before collection or charge-off
6. Accounts closed by the consumer

Review credit reports

Out-of-date

1. Any paid-off civil judgments, collections, repossessions
2. Account balances significantly lower than stated
3. Later pays assumed as recent that are older than 12 months
4. Information older than seven years/10 years for bankruptcy
5. Closed accounts listed as open
6. Paid-off accounts listed with balances
7. Failure to show tax liens have been released

Inaccurate information

1. Incorrect spelling of name/missing or added generation; e.g., Jr. II
2. Inaccurate address (previous five years)

3. Incorrect phone number, Social Security number, employment

4. Accounts listed more than once

5. Account you closed that doesn't say "closed by consumer"

6. Accounts not yours

7. Lawsuits in which you were not involved

8. Late payments that you paid on time (need proof)

9. Name of former spouse still on report

10. Accounts you never opened

11. Inquiries for loans you never authorized

Missing information

- Any debts you pay on time that are not listed
- Positive credit items that are not provided

Select items to dispute on your credit report
Tips:

- Don't bombard credit bureaus with dispute letters one right after another.
- Use the right letter that fits the disputed item. (e.g.,—not mine vs. not late).
- Make sure you tell them your desired outcome.
- Provide reasons for dispute.
- Provide documentation (receipts, cancelled checks, court forms, account statements, landlord paid-in-full letter, etc.). Send copies, not originals.
- Send all disputes by certified mail with return receipts.
- Keep a log of what you send, when you send them, and the responses.

How to Build Good Credit

Even with your credit repaired and paying everything on time, you may still need to establish good credit!

In order to build good credit you should contact two or three loan sources. Due to your credit rating, you probably will need to go to high-risk lenders. They may charge high interest rates (often 24 percent). This is okay short-term as long as you don't borrow much and frequently pay it back. These will probably be secured accounts.

Secured accounts are accounts where you have money securing the payment. Only go for a limit of $200 to $300. This is all you need to build good credit. You don't need any higher borrowing capability. As a matter of fact, don't take a higher loan limit even if they offer it to you!

During this year, borrow a few times against these accounts and make absolutely sure you pay them back on time and not late so it helps you gain good credit scores. When you get the two to three new lines of credit, you will need to notify the three credit bureaus that you have new accounts. We can help you do this.

You may have to use cable, utility, or phone bill payment records to build good credit. Therefore, make sure you pay these on time as well.

Credit dispute log

Name _____

Creditor Bureau _____

Mail _____ Phone _____

Date _____

Item(s) Disputed _____

Response Date_____

Response _____

Buying the Right Kinds and Level of Insurance

Types of insurance you may need

1. Home or renters'
2. Auto
3. Health
4. Life—whole life vs. term insurance
5. Disability
6. Long term care

Get, at the least, annual quotes. Compare rates with a higher deductible.

Maintaining Appropriate Levels of Insurance Coverage

Health insurance

Everyone needs it. You absolutely have to have at least catastrophic coverage for major illness. Only buy this until you can afford full coverage.

The way to keep premiums low is to have higher deductibles. Make sure you have reserves to cover the deductible. Check insurance companies for rates at least annually.

Car insurance

Legally you have to carry car insurance if you own and drive a car. If you have a lien on the car, the insurance company usually tells you how much insurance you need. You do have some options for full coverage; you should ask your insurance agent about your options.

Once the car has low value and is paid for you should check into carrying less coverage such as personal liability and property damage only, as your car ages, it has little value.

Always check different insurance companies at least once per year for rates. Your premiums can be lower if you have a higher deductible, have a good driving record, and, in some states, have a high credit score.

Also check with your insurance company to see if you are in a work group that has lower rates. The value of your car determines the rate, so if you drive a cheaper car and one not rated as a sports type your rate will be lower. Consider this when you buy your next car or if you have teenagers nearing the driving age.

Life insurance

You should have life insurance with two goals.

- First, to cover the cost of a funeral and/or burial.
- Second, to provide your family with enough coverage to replace your income as needed. This can be a large-enough policy to pay off debts or enough to buy income-producing assets.

Never buy life insurance to improve the financial lifestyle of your family or to make them wealthy. If you calculate most life insurance premiums for return on investment or interest paid you will see that they are not good investments. They should be used for protection only. Save the extra money for what you absolutely need and invest it in other assets with a better return. Term insurance in almost every case is cheaper and better than whole life.

Your goal is to get out of debt and build assets so you have future income and don't need much life insurance as you age.

> *Cover only what you need and don't become insurance-poor.*

If you have a mortgage on a home you are buying you will have to keep adequate home insurance. Always make sure you pay it on time and that it doesn't lapse, because your mortgage company will issue very expensive coverage. Once your home is free and clear of debt make sure you have enough insurance protection.

Disability insurance

This is a type of insurance you should check into. It is usually costly. When you can afford it, you should only be covered to the level of replacing needed income in the event you can't work. The best way to avoid needing a high level of disability insurance is to pay off your debts, keep expenses as low as practical, and build up reserves and income-producing assets.

Gap insurance may be cheaper for covering a short amount of time away from work.

When buying insurance always check with more than one company and get quotes at least once per year. Only buy the kind and level of insurance that you need. If you are at this point and want to accelerate your transition, check out our Web site at *www.creatingmoneyforlife.com.*

Challenges to Overcome While Living in the Healthy Lifestyle

The following challenges or roadblocks need to be overcome to be successful in the healthy lifestyle and have a smooth transition to the prosperity lifestyle.

- Keep the emotional desire until the behaviors become habits. You must get over fear of investing or you will never leave the healthy stage. Get help in learning how to build your strategy for creating future income. Avoid looking at and spending money on get-rich-quick schemes. Get the education you need for reading and improving your credit score. Learn to protect your assets. Stop listening to naysayer friends and relatives who will scare you from taking the risks to grow. Convert from holding a major portion of depreciating assets to appreciating assets. Develop the courage to change.
- You will need to change your awareness of and lack of being frugal. You must believe that living slightly below your means is the path to a better life.
- You will have to be passionate about staying on track for reaching your goals. At this level you will most likely need to begin looking for income-producing opportunities and appreciating assets such as investments.
- During the healthy lifestyle you will need to learn how to use and implement many new financial tools to be successful.
- In order to progress to the prosperity lifestyle you must not become complacent just because you're in

a comfort zone. In the healthy lifestyle you will experience less stress from financial shortages and
therefore must avoid being too comfortable.

- You will need to get passionate about building and
maintaining good credit. You will have to take on
the tedious task of disputing any inaccurate information on your credit report.
- Another challenge is to break any conservative attitudes so you can take the necessary risks to advance
your financial position.
- You must see yourself as running a business.
- You will need to stay determined in order to grow to
the next lifestyle: prosperity. You will begin to do tax
planning.
- You will have to overcome the fear of making investment mistakes or fear of losing what you have in
order to turn yourself and your expenses into a business. See how your income is not all yours to spend.
Most of it, except for your allowance, will be allocated to its highest and best use. Learn to run your
finances with the three financial tools a successful
and profitable business uses.
- You will need to alter your mind-set so you enjoy
saving money, paying off debt, and investing. You
must establish and live with short-, medium-, and
long-term financial goals.
- You must learn to push yourself and stay consistent
with new behaviors and, at the same time, create patience. You will have to understand that this process
will take time and effort to be highly successful.
- Calculate, understand, and get excited over growing
your net worth. You must commit to finding the

extra money needed to greatly accelerate your debt payoff plan so you have the money to advance your invest portfolio. You will have to work on raising your confidence for risk taking.

- You must create enough reserves to overcome periods of negative cash flow, especially for those who invest in a business or real-estate venture. For these you need reserves.
- You will need to be in control enough to have cash flow to expand your investment portfolio without taking huge risks.
- You must develop the passion to create passive income and stop working for every penny you have.
- You have to believe you will become wealthy if you keep progressing in your mind-set, your changes, your knowledge, and your actions.
- You must start being less fearful of challenges and look forward to growing through the ones you will face in the future.
- Make sure you are tracking your results for reaching your goals. By reaching your goals, you will be able to set higher level goals. This will take you to high lifestyle levels.

Chapter TEN

The Prosperity Lifestyle

Here are the typical characteristics of those living in the prosperity level.

- They have income that is 50 percent to 100 percent more than what they need to pay their bills. They may have a house payment. If so, it represents a small balance compared to the value of the house. It will have a low interest rate.
- They have zero credit card debt.
- They will grow their net worth every year by increasing assets.
- They take some risk when it comes to investing. However, they have the extra reserves and income to offset any losses.
- Their only other debts are loans on appreciating and income-producing assets.
- They are able and willing to put away 25–50 percent of their income for investments. They are good at

setting and meeting financial goals. Many are entre-
preneurial in spirit and become self-employed. They
enjoy being independent. They are meticulous bud-
geters.

- They know when and where money "leaks" occur.
  They want to plug all leaks.
- Their ego is moving away from having an influence
  on their purchasing. They are climbing the wealth
  ladder and don't have the ego needs of showing off
  financially. They are fine with keeping their cars
  eight to ten years. They take advantage of every tax
  break they can. They spend more time than the
  healthy group focusing on investing. They also
  spend more time on planning for the future. They
  stay focused on moneymaking and asset-building
  opportunities.
- In the prosperity lifestyle many people either buy,
  start, or expand a business venture.
- They develop a different vocabulary—e.g., ROI, dis-
  counting, time value of money, LTV, capital gains,
  depreciation, appreciation, net worth, cash flow,
  pay-back time, assets, liabilities, profit and loss.
- They start to look for multiple streams of income.
  They are getting over the fear of investing.
- Their assets create part of the income that they use
  to accelerate their asset-purchasing plan in order to
  create more income. They watch their return on investments frequently. They have learned to compare
  and contrast opportunities. They gather quotes and
  information and they buy after they do diligence
  through research. They surround themselves with
  other people who have values of being prosperous.

They have fully turned debt-payment dollars into investment dollars.

- They frequently use professionals such as attorneys, accountants, tax planners and investment specialists to get information. They read about money and investing, and frequently talk to their friends about what they are doing financially, but not about how much money or assets they have. They have plenty of cash reserves to cover any emergency, except possibly for long term care.

- Those who want to grow rapidly invest in real estate. They make more logical investments than emotional ones. They are more careful and do more research than the healthy group. They listen to their own internal safeguards rather than salespeople. They have developed the courage to take advantage of opportunities. They think bigger by seeing the whole picture. They look farther down the road into their future. They constantly read about the investments they are excited about and learn how to make better buying decisions. They listen to experts but make the most of their own buying decisions.

The Mind-set of Those Living in the Prosperity Lifestyle

You will need to understand and be willing to change your mind-set. This includes what you frequently think about, what worries you most, how you think, what motivates you, what you read and study, and how you handle stress.

People in the prosperity lifestyle worry about regressing to a lower level by losing their money. Their stress comes from fear of being sued or making bad investment decisions. They stay focused on gain. They look for investments. At this level people have a tendency to worry about future needs. However, they feel good about doing something about it.

Rewards the Prosperity Lifestyle Participants Enjoy

They have financial peace of mind. They are in control enough to alter their financial situation when desired. They have ego feed from having investment knowledge. They can forecast their financial future.

They have fun watching their assets and unearned income grow. Financial stress can be gone for those who can relax. Some, no matter how much money or assets they have in reserve, will still worry. But they don't worry daily about their job as the sole source of income. So they don't concentrate on the importance of payday. They feel good about having more discretionary dollars from spending money on debt payments. They also enjoy paying less taxes due to planning and investing. They like the use of financial strategies to be in control.

Required Lessons for Success in the Prosperity Lifestyle

- You will want to learn more about the economy and financial investments.
- You will need to learn how to develop a quality investing strategy. Learn how to test it, in addition to

learning how to control your habits so you stay focused on it.

- You will need to learn how to develop and implement asset-protection systems.
- You will need to learn how to interview, select, and use professionals for advice, but not overlisten or overpay.
- You will need to acquire the knowledge of a diversified investment portfolio.
- You need to invest in many diverse opportunities and accept you will make some bad decisions and experience loss.
- You will learn more about tax deductions, shelters, and credits. Set up a team of professionals from which to get advice in investing, tax shelters, financial planning, asset protection, etc.
- You will learn to calculate an expected ROI (return on investment).
- You will need to learn the advantages of how to use leverage and compound your investing strategy and any loans you make to others.
- You will learn how to properly acquire and manage real estate investments.

Actions Needed to be Successful in the Prosperity Lifestyle

1. Continue to function as a highly profitable business. Schedule time for monthly reviews of actions and results.

2. As soon as debts are eliminated, transfer the payment money into your investment portfolio.

3. Look for ways to take advantage of more tax credits and deductions.

4. Establish your criteria for making the decision of whether to invest or pass on opportunities you find. Establish yourself as one looking for investment opportunities.

5. Set smart goals; plan for future income needs and steps you need to take to become financially free.

6. Spend time each week reading books and articles about investing.

7. Set aside time weekly to review investment opportunities.

8. Educate yourself about compounding interest, the use of leverage and tax shelters.

9. Interview professionals you will need on your investing advisory team, such as accountants and lawyers.

10. Start to write an investment plan based on the income you forecast you will need and want for the future. Include your mission statement and smart goals. Address the benchmarks, such as activities and deadlines for achieving those goals.

11. Decrease your life and disability insurance as your finances warrant.

12. Borrow in order to buy appreciating assets when it fits your buying strategy and screening criteria.

13. Continue to improve your credit.

14. Do quarterly tax planning.

15. Strongly consider starting or purchasing a business if it fits your plans.

16. Set aside a scheduled timed to review and manage your finances. Avoid doing it only when you get around to it!

17. Start or continue to invest at a faster pace.

18. Develop a network for advice and opportunity awareness.

Information and Ideas for Implementing the Actions Needed to be Successful in the Prosperity Lifestyle

In the prosperity lifestyle the goal is to acquire assets that will create income. I am a strong advocate of using real estate investing as a strategy.

Thanks to leverage, you can control/own real estate with little of your own money. One of our investor clients has approximately $45,000 a year gross family income and owns 10 houses, half of which he bought with 5 percent down and the rest with 10 percent down. In this market an investor with good credit can buy with zero down by using a conventional mortgage.

The advantage of using leverage is that a property appreciates, say, 8 percent, and the investor gets advantage of the entire gain not related to the amount of money put down. For example, if an investor buys a single-family home for $150,000 and it appreciates 8 percent the first year, the new home value would be $162,000. The equity gain of $12,000 would belong to the investor. If the investor put 10 percent down, or $15,000, the return on that cash would be 80 percent. This, of course, in real life wouldn't be as good because it is calculated before taxes, selling and closing costs. If done with a plan, the selling cost can be greatly reduced and the taxes can be deferred through a 1031 exchange or eliminated through a Roth IRA.

The practical look at real estate investing is as follows: You must get some education first. I like buying single-family homes since the management headaches are minimized. You need to have some cash reserves to cover vacancy and redecorating. You can invest in real estate to do what you need to do in your financial plans. For instance, if you need immediate cash flow or to quickly build investment and reserve dollars you can buy and sell (Flip) properties either retail or wholesale. If you are financially healthy and don't need immediate cash flow, you can buy with little money down and hold the properties for appreciation gain.

Most of our clients have a goal of being able to retire in 10 years. If you have savings for reserves and good credit you can accomplish the 10-year goal with one of the two following strategies. The first strategy is to buy two houses per year for the first six years. Hold them for 10 years and then sell half of the houses and keep the remaining six houses. If you buy nice houses in nice neighborhoods and buy them below market price you can keep the rents down and attract good solid tenants. You won't have bad tenant or toilet problems, especially if you set and communicate your rules before the tenants take possession. With common-sense rules remember: It's your house and your rules. Most new investors are scared of the management and midnight calls. With single-family homes there are usually few problems. The economy and loss of a job can cause some late-pay problems. Have a system, use an attorney, be strong in following it, and you will succeed quickly.

Real estate with its high return potential is a great way to catch up if you are behind in your retirement needs program.

Strategy one: Buy 2 houses per year for 6 years. Starting the 10th year sell the house you have held the longest and keep the other one you bought that year. Pay off the mortgage on the second home from the proceeds.

10 Year Program Which Will Create Income for Life

(Calculated at 8 percent appreciation)

Year 1   Buy 2 $130,000

Year 2   Buy 2 $140,000

Year 3   Buy 2 $151,200

Year 4   Buy 2 $163,296

Year 5   Buy 2 $176,359

Year 6   Buy 2 $190,467

Year 7

Year 8

Year 9

Year 10

Value	$280,659	279,860	279,860	279,860	279,860	279,859
Selling Cost	$20,720	22,388	22,388	22,388	22,388	22,388
Mortgage Payoff	$114,042	125,211	137,618	151,011	165,469	181,076
Cash Out	$145,897	132,261	119,854	106,461	92,003	76,393
Pay Off Home 2	$114,042	125,211	137,618	151,011	165,469	181,076
Cash Reserve	$31,855	7,050	(17,764)	(44,550)	(73,466)	(104,681)
Amount Financed	$17,764	44,550	73,466	104,681		
Annual Income from Rent	0	$12,000	$24,000	$36,000	$48,000	$60,000

Note: You must have reserves for holding costs and negative cash flow for the first two years of the mortgage. It is a good idea to use the monthly cash flow to pay down the mortgages faster. But first keep enough reserves.

The second strategy is to buy two houses a year for five years, hold them for 10 years, and sell all of them the 10th through the 15th year (see example below). If you lived on $50,000 per year from the sales and invested the remaining gain in mutual funds or municipal bonds at a 6 percent return you would have all the money you ever need without touching the principal.

Two Houses Per Year Cash-out Program

You must create enough assets to qualify for zero down mortgages and keep credit rating high.

Year 1 buy 2 130,000 sell both homes in Year 11—before-tax profit = $291,794

Year 2 buy 2 140,000 sell both homes in Year 12—before-tax profit = $310,512

Year 3 buy 2 151,200 sell both homes in Year 13—before-tax profit = $335,352

Year 4 buy 2 163,296 sell both homes in Year 14—before-tax profit = $362,180

Year 5 buy 2 176,359 sell both homes in Year 15—before-tax profit = $391,156

This was calculated with an appreciation rate of 8 percent, which is normal for most areas of the country. You need to buy nice houses in nice neighborhoods.

Other keys to being successful in real estate investing are to properly screen tenants, use credit checks, criminal background checks, two former landlord reviews, current residence visitation, budget analysis to make sure they can handle the payment, last two years' tax returns, current income paycheck slips, visit the prospects' home, get enough security deposit as legal, and set, communicate, and stick with your rules. By keeping your rental prices down you can be picky and will attract good, solid tenants. Your goal is to have them pay on time, keep the home up and stay for a long time. But remember to inch the rent up a little each year.

The previous two strategies are the buy and hold strategies. Real estate investing also includes wholesaling junkers, retailing fixer-uppers, buying foreclosures, buying paper, taking control with options, and my favorite—lease options. You can make a lot of money with any of these if you know what you are doing. You must have reserves, funding, knowledge, and good credit. You can do any of the investment strategies by using private lenders, in which case your credit may not be an issue. You can make thousands of dollars per transaction it you know how. Get some help the first few times and roll your plan out. You don't have to have toilet and tenant problems if you have the knowledge, and follow the example of an experienced real estate investor. For guidance, go to www.creatingmoneyforlife.com

Challenges You Will Face During the Prosperity Lifestyle

The following challenges will have to be met in order to be successful in the prosperity lifestyle and to enjoy a smooth transition to the wealthy lifestyle.

You will need to create the interest and skills in finding and analyzing potential investments. You will have to establish an investment strategy to assist you in avoiding random investing. A diversified portfolio is usually best; however, you don't want a mishmash of investment vehicles. You need a balanced variety to offset the times your investments aren't doing well. You should invest in the areas you know.

Another challenge is for you to fine-tune your finances to make sure you have them well organized and managed as a highly profitable business—not merely a growing balance sheet, but good ROI (Return on Investment) and plenty of cash flow.

A balanced portfolio should create multiple streams of income, of which most will be passive income-producing. You should not panic, but develop the sense to quickly cut losses when you have nonperforming investments. In that light you also need to avoid reaction-type investment portfolio changes. Don't sell or buy too fast. Develop a sense of timing for getting in and getting out of investments.

You will need to understand the value of using leverage. Use it in your investing but make sure you have the reserves in place to protect your cash flow and assets. You will need to take risks in investing, but avoid making major mistakes. You will do best by keeping your ego and emotions out of the buying process.

You will need to guard against becoming too complacent with your investments as the world changes every day.

You will need to do tax planning to avoid overpaying taxes and giving up much of your gain.

You will have to control your attitude to avoid being too independent until you develop the investing skills needed. Arrogance created by minimal investing success can lead to disaster. If you start or buy an existing business, you have to buy the size of business that is right for you, at the right time, at the right price, offers the right cash flow and profit, and have the right level of marketing and management in place to ensure success.

Make sure your passive income—which you will need to use for investing to the wealthy level—is not used for personal expenses or consumption.

The final challenge during the prosperity lifestyle is to decide whether you want to become a recreational investor or a professional level investor. In Real Estate one can do very well with a few investments each year. However, there is huge potential for those who decide to become extremely wealthy. The professional investor will have to extend a deeper commitment to their education and skill development. They will have to invest more time. The following self rating sheet will provide you with the skills and education you will need in order to be highly successful.

Professional Real Estate Investing Self Rating

Rate yourself on your skill and knowledge level for each of the following. 1 = very low and 10 being extremely high.

1. Marketing for opportunities   1   2   3   4   5   6   7   8   9   10

2. Advertise for opportunities   1   2   3   4   5   6   7   8   9   10

3. Screen and handle calls   1   2   3   4   5   6   7   8   9   10

4. Analyze deals   1   2   3   4   5   6   7   8   9   10

5. Construct offers   1   2   3   4   5   6   7   8   9   10

6. Make offers   1   2   3   4   5   6   7   8   9   10

7. Negotiate deals   1   2   3   4   5   6   7   8   9   10

8. Create financing   1   2   3   4   5   6   7   8   9   10

9. Close the deal   1   2   3   4   5   6   7   8   9   10

10. Market for buyer or T/B   1   2   3   4   5   6   7   8   9   10

11. Advertise for buyer or T/B   1   2   3   4   5   6   7   8   9   10

12. Find, screen, fill house   1   2   3   4   5   6   7   8   9   10

13. Create proper paper work   1   2   3   4   5   6   7   8   9   10

14. Manage the T/B and property   1   2   3   4   5   6   7   8   9   10

15. Set up business systems   1   2   3   4   5   6   7   8   9   10

16. Manage and grow the business   1   2   3   4   5   6   7   8   9   10

17. Develop job descriptions   1   2   3   4   5   6   7   8   9   10

18. Screen, hire and train employees   1   2   3   4   5   6   7   8   9   10

Chapter ELEVEN

The Wealthy Lifestyle

These are the typical characteristics of those living the wealthy financial lifestyle.

- They have at least 100 percent more income than they need each month to pay their bills.
- They may be still working. If they are, it is not for need of income. They have enough passive income to live on for the rest of their lives.
- They have no debt unless it is from investments that are producing income and/or growth.
- They have constant growth of income through their assets, creating more wealth. This has no correlation to their time spent working. Their money is making them money. They have automatic growth in net worth. Their assets are going up in value and they have no liabilities except for appreciating assets. Their appreciating assets are not highly leveraged.
- They buy assets with a strategy in mind. Their assets

create current cash flow, future capital gains, or huge
income for the future. They usually stay with what
they know and are comfortable with in their portfolio. They have diversity in their investment portfolio
with a broad and deep understanding of investments. They are often invested in real estate and
business ventures. They walk away from question-
able investment opportunities and therefore have
less risky investments. Some of them have huge expenses— they are the ones who live the lifestyle of
the rich. They have many summer homes, jets, etc.
Our definition of wealthy is for those who have
extra income and enjoy having money way beyond
their needs—but may not want the life of luxury or
attention.

• They spend time making decisions about donating
their money or transferring their assets to their
heirs, paying as little in taxes as legally required.
They never have to work again. They have accumulated enough assets producing unearned income.
They are financially free. They have high asset-building goals and the knowledge and skills to reach those
goals.

• They have accumulated a high net worth that pro-
duces enough income to fulfill all of their needs and
more. They are wealth- not possession-focused.
They listen to advice but make their own investment
decisions. They have patience when it comes to investing. They take advantage of tax planning, credits,
and incentives. They have the education to keep
building wealth and can reproduce that behavior.
Their assets create more income and offer opportu-

nities for additional wealth building. They know
how to research and ask the right questions before
they make investing decisions. They share investing
ideas with friends. They have developed and stay
within their investing guidelines. They have developed good investment instincts.

The Mind-set of Those in the Wealthy Lifestyle

You will need to understand and be willing to change your
mind-set. This includes what you frequently think about, what
worries you most, how you think, what motivates you, and
how you handle stress. That comes with wealth.

People living in the wealthy lifestyle worry most about how
to protect and grow their assets. They also worry about what to
do with their money. They see buying and investing through
extremely frugal eyes. They don't worry about money. They
know they can easily replace the assets they have in the event
they lose them all, because they have the knowledge and skills
to create wealth all over again. They have learned to make
money when they need it. If they lost their money, within a
short time they would have it back.

Those in the wealthy lifestyle stay focused on looking for
investments and tax shelters. They don't believe in luck and
they don't buy lottery tickets—they see them as a bad investment. They are somewhat concerned about asset protection
and how they will pass on their wealth to their heirs without
paying high taxes or hurting their children.

Rewards for Living the Wealthy Financial Lifestyle

The wealthy lifestyle people have peace of mind and know that money will never be a worry. Subsequently, they can live financially free forever. They can go where they want, buy whatever they want, and stay as long as they want.

Lessons Needed for the Wealthy Lifestyle

You will need to learn about asset protection. You need to learn how to legally shift your assets to whoever your successor will be, heirs or charities.

Depending on your personality, you may need to learn how to better delegate so you can take some quality time for yourself and family. Some wealthy people are obsessed with making money.

If you own a business or businesses you may want to learn how to screen, train, and evaluate employees and relatives who will be replacing you in the management areas.

Actions Needed to be Successful in the Wealthy Lifestyle

1. Continue to function financially as a well-managed, profitable business.

2. Schedule monthly reviews of all financial instruments, including activities and results of net worth building. Review your balance sheet, profit and loss statements, cash flow results an your investment portfolio.

3. Allocate time to spend on asset protection to make sure your plans are working.

4. Continue to invest in high-return opportunities and those which create more passive income, tax shelter, and appreciation.

5. Cut out life insurance, etc.

6. Establish a plan for transferring your assets, whether to your heirs or donations to charities.

7. Stay connected spiritually by passing some of your wealth forward and helping others.

8. Make sure you spend much of your time in activities you truly enjoy. You have made it financially, don't spend all your time on business and financial management activities.

9. Set up systems for wealth management and estate planning. Depending on the amount of your net worth and assets, you may have to complete multi-generational estate planning.

10. Help heirs prepare for inheritance.

Information and Ideas for Implementing the Actions Needed to be Successful During the Wealth Lifestyle

It is a good idea at this stage to get involved with a peer education group, to gain ideas on managing your wealth, investing for life and estate planning. The ideas will come from group sharing experiences and speakers.

Other resources are schools and individual businesses offering classes to the wealthy. *The Wall Street Journal* recently had an article about the rich going back to school and listed sources for learning how to be rich. The programs listed were IFF Advisors, New York University School of Continuing and Professional Studies' Certificate of Wealth Management, Tiger 21, University of Chicago Graduate School of Business, University of Miami Continuing and International Education's Preserving and Transferring Wealth, and University of Pennsylvania Wharton School/Institute for Private Investors.

Challenges to Living the Wealthy Lifestyle

You will need to develop proper systems for protecting your assets. In addition, you will need to have knowledge and professional advice to avoid paying more taxes than legally necessary. This can be done sometimes by investing in the right vehicles and sometimes by controlling when you buy and sell.

You will need to keep your anonymity and stay out of the public eye as a wealthy person to avoid being vulnerable to crime. You will need protection against family and friends who ask to borrow or take your money.

You must avoid getting your ego involved with financial growth and investments to avoid not knowing when to slow down and spend quality time with family and friends.

Another challenge is to avoid building an empire—creating stress and a time trap you have trouble getting away from. You will need to learn about estate planning and wealth-management techniques.

You may have to create hobbies and activities you will enjoy if you spend too much time creating wealth.

Chapter TWELVE

The Conclusion

I sincerely hope you enjoyed this book. I hope it has given you a whole new perspective on which lifestyle you are living and what you can do if you want to change. My goal is to have every reader understand and have a feel for the differences in how people think, what they think about, and the actions they take for each of the five financial lifestyles. You now have a roadmap to follow all the way to the wealthy lifestyle. In order for me to be successful as a nonfiction educational writer I need to have met the six main missions for which I wrote this book.

Mission No. 1: To assist you in knowing which lifestyle you are currently living. Before reading this book I am sure you had a feeling for how you were doing, but couldn't relate it to real lifestyles. By actually comparing actions/habits and financial knowledge you have a more definitive view. You should now be able to identify with what higher-level lifestyle people know, think, and do. You also know what behavior modifications you must make to change your lifestyle. This will help you make the decision to stay where you are or go for the gold.

Mission No. 2: To provide a wake-up call for those who are drifting, suffering financially, or living happily in the healthy lifestyle and don't realize the trap they are heading for. Now is your opportunity to take control and intervene.

Mission No. 3: To offer you a means to jump-start your change to the next higher level. If you want more, the information here should be a catalyst to get you started. Don't hesitate for fear of the unknown or not knowing what to do. You have the steps—go for it.

Mission No. 4: To provide you with the total step-by-step process to get you from where you are to where you want to be in the shortest time possible. As you progress, use this book as your guide. Review the behaviors, thoughts, challenges, and information to prepare you for what to do next. As your confidence, courage, and passion for improvement grow you will see that all the lessons you need are here.

Mission No. 5: To inspire you to reach out to others with this education, help others enjoy their financial futures, which will have a strong impact on the pride in America. Make sure you offer this information to your children. Don't let them become part of the 70% living paycheck to paycheck.

Mission No. 6: To have you enjoy the book. I hope the seriousness of the content was delivered in such a way that you want to keep reading and learn more. I hope it has been an educational, informational, fun, enlightening experience. Thank you again for caring enough about you financial future to do something. If it was of value to you, please pass it along to help others.

The mission I presented in the beginning was to have you know the path to wealth. It can only be achieved by your intervention. The intervention will come about when you have the desire to change and empower yourself to make the change happen. To develop through the lifestyles until you reach wealth takes commitment, know-how, and action. By learning the lessons and taking the actions presented in this book for each level you can reach any financial goals you set.

In order to change your lifestyle you must alter your habits. To do that you will need to know what you want to change, what your old habits are, create a strong enough reason to change, know what you need to know to change, know what behaviors it will take to change, practice those new behaviors, get over the challenges, resist regressing, recognize and enjoy rewards for your progress, and stick with the new behaviors until they become your new habits. It is time for you to decide if you want change or not. If you do take what you have learned, use this book for reference and apply it, you will become whatever you desire.

You are not in this alone in your journey; we are here to help. Visit *www.creatingmoneyforlife.com.* Godspeed.

About the Author

The author, Denny Bowersox, holds a bachelor's degree in sociology and psychology from Western Michigan University and a master's degree in counseling from Central Michigan University. He has taught psychology, personal finance, business, profitability, and leadership. Denny has started and run profitable small businesses as well as teaching for six colleges and universities (Western Michigan University, Kalamazoo College, Davenport College, Wayne State University, Glenn Oakes College and Kalamazoo Valley). He has had training contracts with the State of Michigan Commerce Department. His company, Financial Health Systems LLC, is qualified in all fifty states to supply debtor education through the U.S. Trustees Program under the Department of Justice for the required course under the bankruptcy laws.

Denny has also been a business consultant for the state of Michigan under the "Growth Margin Program," Economic Development Small Business division, for helping entrepreneurs grow their cash flow, profitability, and business success.

The two corporations (New Path Homes, Inc., and Financial Health Systems LLC) he currently owns help individuals with their budget and credit issues in order to become homeowners. This function falls under his real estate Broker's license, with a specialty in real estate investing and management. Personal finances and real estate investment education courses are also provided through these entities.

In previous years Denny functioned in many leadership roles: operations manager of a large pharmaceutical company (Perrigo), president of his church, chairman of a planning commission, chairman of the local public school system's Booster Club, vice president of the Gull Lake Community Schools school board, and president of the Battle Creek Landlords Association.

Additionally, Denny has purchased or started six profitable small businesses, which include Snappy Oil Change, Bowersox & Associate Consulting, PIP Printing franchise, Lease Option Homes Real estate Investments Inc., Business Success Center - Education and Training; and Bowersox and Kluger Real Estate Management Company. His excitement is derived from the hope of sharing his past experiences through this book, and that it becomes an inspiration for helping anyone who is willing to intervene and bring about financial peace and prosperity into their lives.